Welcome to College Prowler®

During the writing of College Prowler's guidebooks, we felt it was critical that our content was unbiased and unaffiliated with any college or university. We think it's important that our readers get honest information and a realistic impression of the student opinions on any campus—that's why if any aspect of a particular school is terrible, we (unlike a campus brochure) intend to publish it. While we do keep an eye out for the occasional extremist—the cheerleader or the cynic—we take pride in letting the students tell it like it is. We strive to create a book that's as representative as possible of each particular campus. Our books cover both the good and the bad, and whether the survey responses point to recurring trends or a variation in opinion, these sentiments are directly and proportionally expressed through our guides.

College Prowler guidebooks are in the hands of students throughout the entire process of their creation. Because you can't make student-written guides without the students, we have students at each campus who help write, randomly survey their peers, edit, layout, and perform accuracy checks on every book that we publish. From the very beginning, student writers gather the most up to date stats, facts, and inside information on their colleges. They fill each section with student quotes and summarize the findings in editorial reviews. In addition, each school receives a collection of letter grades (A through F) that reflect student opinion and help to represent contentment, prominence, or satisfaction for each of our 20 specific categories. Just as in grade school, the higher the mark the more content, more prominent, or more satisfied the students are with the particular category.

Once a book is written, additional students serve as editors and check for accuracy even more extensively. Our bounce-back team—a group of randomly selected students who have no involvement with the project—are asked to read over the material in order to help ensure that the book accurately expresses every aspect of the university and its students. This same process is applied to the 200-plus schools College Prowler currently covers. Each book is the result of endless student contributions, hundreds of pages of research and writing, and countless hours of hard work. All of this has led to the creation of a student information network that stretches across the nation to every school that we cover. It's no easy accomplishment, but it's the reason that our guides are such a great resource.

When reading our books and looking at our grades, keep in mind that every college is different and that the students who make up each school are not uniform—as a result, it is important to assess schools on a case-by-case basis. Because it's impossible to summarize an entire school with a single number or description, each book provides a dialogue, not a decision, that's made up of 20 different topics and hundreds of student quotes. In the end, we hope that this guide will serve as a valuable tool in your college selection process. Enjoy!

OMID GOHARI ○ CHRISTINA KOSHZOW ○ CHRIS MASON ○ JOEY RAHIMI ○ LUKE SKURMAN ○
The College Prowler Team

Syracuse University
Syracuse, New York

Written by Steve Krakauer

*Edited by Adam Burns, Kristin Burns, Kimberly Moore,
Jon Skindzier, and Tim Williams*

Layout by Matt Hamman

*Additional contributions by Omid Gohari,
Christina Koshzow, Chris Mason, Joey Rahimi,
and Luke Skurman*

ISBN # 1-4274-0143-8
ISSN # 1552-0749

Last Updated 5/15/06

Special Thanks To: Babs Carryer, Andy Hannah, LaunchCyte, Tim O'Brien, Bob Sehlinger, Thomas Emerson, Andrew Skurman, Barbara Skurman, Bert Mann, Dave Lehman, Daniel Fayock, Chris Babyak, The Donald H. Jones Center for Entrepreneurship, Terry Slease, Jerry McGinnis, Bill Ecenberger, Idie McGinty, Kyle Russell, Jacque Zaremba, Larry Winderbaum, Roland Allen, Jon Reider, Team Evankovich, Lauren Varacalli, Abu Noaman, Mark Exler, Daniel Steinmeyer, Jared Cohon, Gabriela Oates, David Koegler, and Glen Meakem.

Bounce-Back Team: Jon Adler, Ron Levy, and George Azor.

College Prowler®
5001 Baum Blvd.
Suite 750
Pittsburgh, PA 15213

Phone: 1-800-290-2682
Fax: 1-800-772-4972
E-Mail: info@collegeprowler.com
Web Site: www.collegeprowler.com

Table of Contents

Introduction from the Author

Syracuse University may mean different things to different people. To the sports fan, hearing Syracuse will bring up images of SU's championship basketball team and superstars like Carmelo Anthony, Gerry MacNamara, and Hakim Warrick. For others, hearing Syracuse will automatically bring up thoughts of upstate New York and snowy winters.

The true draw of Syracuse University is becoming what is probably the most important part of any college: its academics. SU is ranked among the top 50 colleges in the US, and its prestige is growing. Within SU are many well-renowned individual colleges like Newhouse School of Communications, Architecture, Management and Information Studies. These colleges, as well as the five other SU colleges, are very reputable in the academic community. SU has also made it its goal to become the nation's leading student-centered research university.

Over the past few years, SU has looked to raise its academic standards. As a result, the admittance rate has actually gone down. This means it is more difficult to get into Syracuse University, and the class sizes have dropped, as well. One thing that is never falling off is the rate at which SU builds new buildings and renovates old ones.

If you're interested in SU, you probably already know a little about its academic standing, athletic prowess, and poor weather. You also probably have a lot of questions associated with the school. What is the social scene like? How are the dorms? What are some fun things to do around Syracuse? But, the biggest question you should be asking yourself is a big one: do you want to spend the next four years of your life at SU? Although not an easy question to answer, this book will provide you with valuable, real information from someone who has not only had to make that very decision, but is currently a student at SU. Hopefully, this book will give you the insight you need to decide if Syracuse University is right for you.

Steve Krakauer, Author
Syracuse University

By the Numbers

General Information

Syracuse University
201 Tolley Administration
Building
Syracuse, NY 13244

Control:
Private

Academic Calendar:
Semester

Religious Affiliation:
None

Founded:
1870

Web Site:
www.syr.edu

Main Phone:
(315) 443-1870

Admissions Phone:
(315) 443-3611

Student Body

**Full-Time
Undergraduates:**
11,448

**Part-Time
Undergraduates:**
820

**Total Male
Undergraduates:**
5,270

**Total Female
Undergraduates:**
6,998

Admissions

Overall Acceptance Rate:
59%

Early Decision Acceptance Rate:
63%

Regular Decision Acceptance Rate:
59%

Total Applicants:
16,019

Total Acceptances:
9,463

Freshman Enrollment:
2,671

Yield (% of admitted students who enroll):
28.2%

Early Decision Available?
Yes

Early Action Available?
N/A

Early Decision Deadline:
November 15

Early Decision Notification:
December 30

Regular Decision Deadline:
January 1

Must-Reply-By Date:
May 1

Applicants Placed on Waiting LIst:
883

Applicants Accepted from Waiting List:
256

Students Enrolled from Waiting List:
155

Transfer Applications Recieved:
896

Transfer Applications Accepted:
556

Transfer Students Enrolled:
300

Transfer Application Acceptance Rate:
62%

Common Application Accepted?
Yes

Supplemental Forms?
Yes

Admissions E-Mail:
orange@syr.edu

Admissions Web Site:
admissions.syr.edu

SAT I or ACT Required?
Yes

**SAT I Range
(25th–75th Percentile):**
1120–1320

**SAT Verbal Range
(25th–75th Percentile):**
550–650

**SAT Math Range
(25th–75th Percentile):**
570–670

SAT II Required?
No

Retention Rate:
92%

**Top 10% of
High School Class:**
44%

Application Fee:
$60

Financial Information

Full-Time Tuition:
$28,285

Room and Board:
$10,370

Books and Supplies:
$1,210

**Average Financial Aid
Package:**
$19,200

**Students Who Applied for
Financial Aid:**
67%

**Students Who Received
Financial Aid:**
70%

**Financial Aid Forms
Deadline:**
February 1

Financial Aid Phone:
(315) 443-1513

Financial Aid E-Mail:
finmail@syr.edu

Financial Aid Web Site:
financialaid.syr.edu

Academics

The Lowdown On...
Academics

Degrees Awarded:

Bachelor
Master
Post-Master Certificate
First Professional
Doctorate

Most Popular Majors:

14% Business Management, Marketing
14% Communication, Journalism
14% Social Sciences
12% Visual and Performing Arts
7% Computer/Information Sciences

Undergraduate Schools:

College of Arts and Sciences
College of Human Services and Health Professions
College of Visual and Performing Arts
L.C. Smith College of Engineering and Computer Science
Martin J. Whitman School of Management
S.I. Newhouse School of Public Communications
School of Architecture
School of Education
School of Information Studies

➜

Full-Time Faculty:
879

Faculty with Terminal Degree:
88%

Student-to-Faculty Ratio:
12:1

Graduation Rates:
Four-Year: 66%
Five-Year: 77%
Six-Year: 79%

Average Course Load:
15 credits (5 courses)

Special Degree Options
Many schools, like public communications, arts and sciences, and information studies and management have dual-degree programs that offer joint majors between different colleges.

AP Test Score Requirements
Different for each subject; check *http://admissions.syr.edu/faqs*.

Sample Academic Clubs
Advertising Club, Entrepreneurship Club, Investment Club

Best Places to Study
Bird Library, dorm floor lounges, Panasci lounge

Did You Know?

Newhouse School of Public Communications and the School of Architecture are among **the top colleges in the field in the country.** The School of Management is in the top-40 schools by many rankings in their field. For graduate schools, the Maxwell School of Citizenship is the best school for International Relations and Public Policy in the country.

Syracuse offers a **Technology Classroom Survey** that allows students to share their ideas on improvement. To check it out, go to *www.fcms.syr.edu/classrooms/room_survey.htm*.

Students Speak Out On...
Academics

> "Most of the teachers at SU are understanding and responsive to the students' needs; however, there are a few that are just self-centered and arrogant."

Q "**The teachers vary**. Most are really good, but there are some bad ones. I've taken a lot of interesting electives."

Q "The teachers are willing to work with you, but **you have to make the initial effort and seek them out first**. They are fair in their teaching and easy to get in contact with if you need some additional help with the class. You have your good teachers and your bad teachers. It really just depends on who you get."

Q "My teachers are great; I don't know about all the teachers at this school. **Professors come from all over the place**. Some have even written their own books and use them in class."

Q "In my department, the professors are fantastic and are very well respected within their field. Like at any school, some professors show a greater enthusiasm than others, but overall, the professors are wonderful. Due to my professors' enthusiasm and their ability to challenge us, I really enjoy class. **I came to Syracuse because of its reputation as one of the top architecture schools** in the nation."

Q "The teachers that I've had at SU so far are pretty interesting. Some teachers are much more exciting and interesting than others, but **for the most part, they are informative and stimulating**."

Q "You find teachers that like what they do. **They enjoy the work because they enjoy working with students**. Then, there are others where you can tell that they chose a profession that they have grown to deplore, and they are so dull as individuals that they extend their own karma into their teaching."

Q "**The quality of professors varies wildly**. Sometimes, you'll get an excellent professor, and sometimes you'll get a horrible professor. Pray that you don't get a foreign grad student for a teacher because they can't even speak English well."

Q "The teachers here are marvelous. **They're all very accommodating and available all the time**. But never call your professor a teacher; you'll get on their bad side if you call them that. Some professors are tough, but some are flexible. If you are smart about the way that you approach them, they could give you an extension on the due date for some assignments."

Q "Teachers are knowledgeable, and **some are renowned in their field**. Most classes are interesting and stimulating."

Q "The teachers at Syracuse University are a mixed bag. **Some teachers are excellent, while others are not so good**. Overall, I would say that the teaching here is good. Most teachers are very helpful if you approach them. But there are a few of them, sadly, who lack a personal touch and will not make any extra effort to reach out to you."

The College Prowler Take On...
Academics

Syracuse is a university of choices. SU has over 200 majors in nine undergraduate colleges, so you're bound to find some that are agreeable. A few of SU's schools are world-renowned: the SI Newhouse School of Public Communications, School of Management, and the School of Architecture are premiere programs that house some of the top professors in their specific field. Also, the School of Information Studies and Visual and Performing Arts hold high status, as well.

The faculty at SU is generally compliant with students' needs. All professors must hold office hours during the week, and most instructors conveniently hand out their home numbers, as well. If you make use of the availability of your professors, go to class, do your homework, and study for the big tests, and you should have no problem getting excellent grades. Most classes are interesting, but sometimes you'll get a class with those monotone, lengthy lectures and dread that two hours of rambling each week. Your consolation is that a decent number of professors post their lectures online and don't take attendance. There are the classes with somewhere around 15 to 20 people where you'll receive, more often than not, excellent teaching, and you'll come away with a whole new perspective. Either way, SU learning is quite a bit different—and better—than high school.

B

The College Prowler® Grade on
Academics: B

A high Academics grade generally indicates that professors are knowledgeable, accessible, and genuinely interested in their students' welfare. Other determining factors include class size, how well professors communicate, and whether or not classes are engaging.

Local Atmosphere

The Lowdown On...
Local Atmosphere

Region:
Northeast

City, State:
Syracuse, New York

Setting:
Small City

Distance from NYC:
4 hours

Distance from Montreal:
4 hours

Distance from Buffalo:
2 hours

Points of Interest:
Armory Square
Baseball Hall of Fame
Everson Museum of Art
Turning Stone Casino

➜

Closest Shopping Malls:

Carousel Center Mall
9090 Carousel Center Drive
Syracuse, NY 13290
(315) 466-7000

Shoppingtown Mall
3649 Erie Boulevard East
Dewitt, NY 13214
(315) 446-9160

Major Sports Teams:

Syracuse SkyChiefs
(AAA baseball)

Syracuse Crunch
(minor league hockey)

Closest Movie Theaters:

Regal Cinema
Carousel Mall
(315) 466-5678

Regal Cinema
Shoppingtown Mall
(315) 449-2210

Westcott Cinema
524 Westcott Street
(315) 479-9911

City Web Sites

www.syracuse.com
www.syracuse.ny.us
www.syracusefun.com

Did You Know?

5 Fun Facts about Syracuse:

- The Syracuse State Fair, started in 1841, is **the longest running state fair in the country**.
- **The first traffic light ever made** was manufactured in Syracuse.
- **The candle-making industry began** in Syracuse in 1855.
- Syracuse was **named after Siracusa**, an ancient city in Sicily.
- The person who **invented the device that most shoe stores use to measure** shoe size lived in Syracuse.

Famous Syracusans:

Tom Cruise – Actor

Richard Gere – Actor

Bobcat Goldthwait – Actor

Dave Mirra – BMX biker

Jim Boeheim – Syracuse University men's basketball head coach

Libba Cotton – Grammy Award-winning folk singer

Students Speak Out On...
Local Atmosphere

{ **"The city of Syracuse survives because of SU. Syracuse doesn't have much of a downtown atmosphere, but the bar scene and Greek life make up for this loss."**

Q "There are too many SUNY-ESF kids! There are some Lemoyne kids, but very few. There is a **semi-Greek atmosphere at SU**. You should visit Marshall Street."

Q "There are **a few other universities in the area**, such as Lemoyne, but the town is pretty much known for Syracuse University and only Syracuse University. It's a pretty nice town, but it would be nothing without SU."

Q "Syracuse is a city, so **there are always things to do** and new people to meet. But because it is a big school, you can always entertain yourself on campus. And we have one of the biggest malls in the country nearby!"

Q "The only place to stay away from is the ghetto. If the people who live there see you walking around there, **they won't bother you**, but you need to act confident. Don't be scared."

Q "**Syracuse isn't exactly San Francisco**, but it's not too bad. People are generally nice, and there are other colleges in the area. There are a lot of outdoor things to do, like skiing in the winter or hiking when the weather's warmer."

Q "Lemoyne College is a small liberal arts school, and we rarely, if ever, intermingle with them. **There is a casino about 20 minutes away** on an Indian reservation, and you only have to be 18 to gamble here."

Q "All I can say is **Syracuse is definitely a good time**. The party scene is usually bumping, and even on those slow nights, you can always just kick back, buy a 30-case, and play Madden and beer pong!"

Q "Like at any big university, **the atmosphere in Syracuse is what you make it to be**. Most students are outgoing, and there are enough people here that you're sure to find your niche. Just make sure to steer clear of the herds of sorority girls in their black North Face fleece uniforms."

Q "The atmosphere in Syracuse is pretty nice, I think. Nearby, you have Onondaga Community College and Lemoyne. **Sometimes, you'll run into students from those other schools in bars and stuff**. Niagara Falls isn't far away, either."

Q "**The city is so-so**. There are other universities around, but we don't see much of them. You don't want to get lost around Syracuse at night, but there are some cool places like Armory Square and Carousel Center."

Q "You do have quite a lot to do in Syracuse. **We have the Carousel Mall to brag about**, one of the most complete and largest malls in New York state. If you are a gaming freak, Shoppingtown Mall is the place for you. There are also the outdoor arts and antique shows, annual festivals and fairs, Sunday-night bowling, ice-skating, the Syracuse Zoo, the Jamesville Lake, and so many other exciting places to go to."

Q "**Syracuse is an excellent town to live in**. The atmosphere here is either peaceful or lively depending on where you are. So, whether you're the type who bustles with activity or the peaceful kind of bloke, Syracuse is the place for you!"

The College Prowler Take On...
Local Atmosphere

Whenever discussing Syracuse, it is important to distinguish between the city of Syracuse and the University of Syracuse. Never is it more evident than in this section. SU is the castle on top of the Syracuse hill. Since Syracuse is a large university, most students find contentment in staying on campus because there is usually something going on. For those students that wish to venture off the campus, there are still options for them in the city of Syracuse and the surrounding areas.

There isn't much going on in the actual city of Syracuse; however, Carousel Mall is a popular hangout for SU students. The mall, most of the time, is far more populated by Syracuse high school kids. Then, there is Turning Stone Casino, a quick 30-minute drive from the campus, where students can legally gamble away what little money they have left. You can also bowl, barhop, or catch a movie, again at Carousel Mall. Your best option to get out of the routine for a weekend is to head to Montreal, only a four-hour trip. Also, SU is huge, so seeing a Lemoyne College or Onondaga Community College student on SU's campus is about as rare as a warm front.

B

The College Prowler® Grade on
Local
Atmosphere: B

A high Local Atmosphere grade indicates that the area surrounding campus is safe and scenic. Other factors include nearby attractions, proximity to other schools, and the town's attitude toward students.

Safety & Security

The Lowdown On...
Safety & Security

Public Safety Phone:
(315) 443-2224

Safety Web Site:
http://publicsafety.syr.edu

Safety Services:
Access to recent crime logs
Blue-light phones
Call trace
Campus alerts
Date rape prevention
Neighborhood safety patrol
Shuttle service
Silent Witness program

Health Services:

Allergy injections

Ambulatory care services

Health education and wellness promotion

Laboratory and X-ray services

Nutrition counseling

Office visits

Pharmacy

Public health monitoring and oversight

SU Medical Transport Services (MTS)

Syracuse University Ambulance (SUA)

Health Center:

Syracuse University Health Services

111 Waverly Avenue

http://students.syr.edu/depts/ health/index.html

(315) 443-2666

Emergency Phone: 711 (from a campus phone) or (315) 443-4299

Fax: (315) 443-9190

Health Center Hours:

Monday–Friday 8:30 a.m.– 5 p.m., 24 hours for nurse care

Did You Know?

Many of the **SU ambulance employees are SU students** themselves.

Students Speak Out On...
Safety & Security

{ **"Security and safety is good, but the school security guards are on a serious power trip. They think they are the FBI or something."**

Q "**I've had no problem with safety on campus**. The only time someone I know had anything stolen from him was during move-in day when he left his door unlocked. As long as you take the proper precautions to protect yourself and your stuff, you'll be fine. Public Safety is very prevalent on campus. Often, I leave my studio class at three or four in the morning and have never felt any danger when walking back to my dorm."

Q "Security is okay. They have people who come to the dorms between 8 p.m. and 7 a.m. to check people in and out. There are random campus safety vehicles that are always around, but **if you live off campus, it can get a little sketchy**."

Q "Honestly, **Syracuse is not the safest city in the world**, but it's not the most dangerous city either, and the campus is very safe. Either you have to be a Syracuse University student or you have to be signed in by one in order to get into the dorms."

Q "**I don't usually feel unsafe on campus**, but we are surrounded by a city, and there have been a few incidents after which they did boost security. I recommend going out in a group at night."

Q "There is a blue-light call-box system in place, but obviously, like anywhere, **you shouldn't walk anywhere alone at night**."

Q "Overall, security is pretty good. **They could do more**, but for the most part, the campus is pretty safe."

Q "**Public Safety is an absolute joke**. They prevent nothing. They are unarmed and disrespected, which lowers their potential shot at some kind of authority. All they are good for is busting kids for drinking or smoking in the dorms."

Q "SU has **a Public Safety service, which is separate from the Syracuse Police Department**. SU also has a blue-light phone system. I've never had to use it, though."

Q "You have to live in the dorms for two years, and **security on campus is very good**. There are people who sign you in and check your ID after 8 p.m. As long as you take the right precautions, you'll be fine."

Q "**Public Safety runs a 'Shuttle Home' service**. If any student ever feels that it would be unsafe to walk home, whether from a late class or even from being out late partying, this shuttle provides a ride home."

The College Prowler Take On...
Safety & Security

The area around the Syracuse campus is not the safest place to be at night. Armed robberies that occur on the outskirts of campus are reported almost weekly. Still, the frequency of these instances is on the decline, as SU takes steps to remedy the situation. Recently, Public Safety officers on campus have been converted to "peace officers." This means more jurisdiction and possible armament. (They have firearms!) Still, if you don't walk alone after dark on a few well known and notorious streets, you should stay unharmed during your four years at school. In other words, just use common sense.

One major note—the city of Syracuse displays a strong dissemblance to the campus of Syracuse when discussing safety and security. Although some robberies occur on the outskirts of SU, more serious crimes like shootings, burglaries, and gang activity occur mostly in the inner-city. Just don't venture to that part of the city, especially not alone. Despite the fact that Syracuse is surrounded by a fairly rural area of central New York, it still is a city and has a city-like crime rate. Just be careful, but don't get overly stressed.

The College Prowler® Grade on

Safety & Security: C+

A high grade in Safety & Security means that students generally feel safe, campus police are visible, blue-light phones and escort services are readily available, and safety precautions are not overly necessary.

Computers

The Lowdown On...
Computers

High-Speed Network?
Yes—Ethernet in every dorm room and computer lab.

Wireless Network?
Yes

Number of Labs:
9

Number of Computers:
Over 400 PCs

Operating Systems:
Microsoft Windows XP

Free Software

Adobe software, McAfee antivirus software, Microsoft Office, Web development tools, compilers, and statistics and mathematics software

24-Hour Labs

Five: Brockway, Huntington, Kimmel, Lawrinson, Link

Charge to Print?

500 free black and white sheets per year; color pages are 50 cents per page for standard 8.5" x 11" sheets.

Did You Know?

Consultants are available in **the Kimmel Computer Cluster** until midnight every weeknight to help with any problems you have.

Students Speak Out On...
Computers

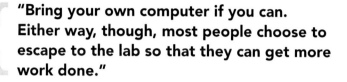

"Bring your own computer if you can. Either way, though, most people choose to escape to the lab so that they can get more work done."

Q "I've only noticed **crowded computer labs during finals**. If you are able to bring your own computer, I would recommend it."

Q "**You need your own computer**. Computer labs are scattered across campus, but they are often busy. You have print credits, but printing at the library costs per sheet."

Q "The computer network could use some help. Connections are often slow and labs are often crowded beyond capacity. A personal computer is a good idea. **The campus has a very good wireless Internet network** that serves most of the campus, and with a laptop, accessing and utilizing the campus's computer resources is a piece of cake."

Q "Definitely bring your own computer. The computer clusters tend to get crowded. Oh yeah, one more thing, **ResNet support is horrible**. They are supposed to be the campus computer technicians, but their practices are very unprofessional."

Q "**The computer labs are good, but it can be a big pain** to have to go the whole way to the nearest computer cluster, especially when the weather sucks. So I would suggest that you bring a computer with you."

Q "Most of the students I've met own their own computers. The computer clusters around campus have been helpful for me because **they are open 24 hours and have a good atmosphere** to complete my work."

Q "I would have brought my own computer if I'd had one. **The labs get pretty crowded during the day**, but at night, they're not too bad."

Q "Some of the computer labs are open 24 hours a day, but **bring your own computer anyway**."

Q "Some of the computer labs here are great, while others simply suck. **The badly-maintained labs are not that fast and do not work properly**. The great labs have computers with excellent speed, efficiency, and network connections."

The College Prowler Take On...
Computers

Most people stress bringing a personal computer, but that is not to say that Syracuse doesn't offer an abundance of resources to its students. With many 24-hour workstations spread around campus, a communal computer is always available for student use. There are really only two reasons you absolutely need your own computer: leisure activities (surfing the Internet, downloading mp3s, talking on Instant Messenger, and playing computer games) or to do your work without trudging through feet of snow. Like most campuses, students basically live on Instant Messenger, and unlike most campuses, it snows a lot.

One reason students have developed a love affair with using Instant Messenger services, as well as wasting all their computer's memory on downloaded music is the incredible Ethernet service that SU provides. It is fast, reliable, and convenient. Be careful, though—if it should malfunction, it could take days to get ResNet to fix it. As for whether you should bring a laptop or a PC, the best choice is a laptop. Having the option of bringing in a project to class on PowerPoint or bringing your work to the library or a lounge on campus is invaluable.

The College Prowler® Grade on

Computers: B

A high grade in Computers designates that computer labs are available, the computer network is easily accessible, and the campus' computing technology is up-to-date.

Facilities

The Lowdown On...
Facilities

Student Center:
Goldstein Student Center
Schine Student Center

Athletic Center:
Archbold Gymnasium
Goldstein Gymnasium

Libraries:
Bird Library
Carnegie Library
Smaller, inter-college libraries

Campus Size:
200 acres

Popular Places to Chill:
Archbold Gym
Eggers Café in Eggers Hall
Panasci Lounge in Schine
Student Center
The Quad (middle of campus)
Studio Break in Slocum Hall

What Is There to Do on Campus?

Shows (comedy and concerts), school-sponsored gym activities, famous speakers

Movie Theater on Campus?

No, although on weekends there are movies played in Watson Theater and Huntington-Beard Crouse Lecture Hall.

Bar on Campus?

No

Bowling on Campus?

No

Coffeehouse on Campus?

Yes, there are two. Perc Place is used for open-mics and concerts and is located in Hendricks Chapel. Jabberwocky Café is open during the day and some evenings and is located in Schine Underground.

Students Speak Out On...
Facilities

> "The gym sucks. It's too crowded, and there are not enough machines. They use very outdated equipment."

 "I can't complain about the facilities on campus. The Schine Student Center has a good dining center, a bookstore, and a large auditorium for various events. **All the computers on campus are updated with the latest operating systems** (Windows XP). The athletic centers are decent; however, I think the weight room could be much better. Most of the equipment is very old, and it tends to be always overcrowded."

"**There is a state-of-the-art gymnasium** on campus that anyone can use, and there are also some great recreational facilities. The student center is good, too—nothing amazing, but it gets the job done."

"The facilities are really nice. The computers are good, **the student center has pretty much everything you could need**, and the gym has a pool and huge weight room. In addition, you can take physical education classes for credit in any sport from golf to kickboxing to horseback riding."

"We've got **a huge gym and lots of computer labs**."

"**All of the facilities at Syracuse are state-of-the-art**. I'm at the gym everyday, and it definitely gets two thumbs up from me! Seriously, though, it rocks."

Q "I can't complain about the facilities on campus. The Schine Student Center has a good dining center, a bookstore, and a large auditorium for various events. **All the computers on campus are updated with the latest operating systems** (Windows XP). Computer clusters are often crammed. Student center? Where? Schine is not nearly big enough to be called a student center."

Q "The student center is nice. It's got a bookstore, a computer lab, a food court, a game room, an auditorium, a student lounge, and a bunch of offices. **The gym isn't great, but it's not horrible**. It's an older gym, and they really need a new one, but they have a lot of treadmills and elliptical machines, so I never had any issues with it."

The College Prowler Take On...
Facilities

If you were to go on a tour of SU, the tour guides would deliberately highlight certain facilities on campus and avoid others. They'd show you every nook and cranny of the Schine Student Center, while merely breezing by Archbold Gymnasium. Schine has a lot to offer: the food court is impressive, the bookstore is great for picking up class materials, and there is a box office for buying tickets to any lectures, concerts, or other shows that pass through the SU campus. Also in Schine is the Panasci Lounge on the second floor—perfect for relaxing, sleeping, studying, or just watching the beautiful scenery of SU during a snowfall. Also in the student center is a coffee lounge, a large auditorium where concerts are held, and a computer lab. The buildings on the campus, especially the older ones, can be breathtaking in their architecture. The Crouse building looks like a castle, and the Hall of Languages is a beautiful piece of history. The buildings of SU epitomize how a college campus should look.

Archbold Gymnasium is quite a bit less appealing for the average student. Although the pool is notable in its size, the actual exercise area is small and located on a converted basketball court. There is a wide selection of treadmills and elliptical machines, but the free weights are sprawled about the gym and the circuit-type machines are all typically being used. A one-hour workout can turn into a two-hour affair simply because of the lack of equipment and organization.

B+

The College Prowler® Grade on
Facilities: B+

A high Facilities grade indicates that the campus is aesthetically pleasing and well maintained, and that facilities are state-of-the-art. Other determining factors include the quality of both athletic and student centers, and an abundance of things to do on campus.

Campus Dining

The Lowdown On...
Campus Dining

Freshman Meal Plan Requirement?
Yes

Meal Plan Average Cost:
$2,200 per semester

Places to Grab a Bite With Your Meal Plan:

Blinker Snack Bar
Food: Breakfast foods, bagels, sandwiches
Location: HBC building
Hours: Monday–Friday 7:45 a.m.–2:30 p.m.

→

Brockway Dining Hall

Food: Breakfast, lunch, dinner

Location: Brockway Hall

Hours: Monday–Friday
7 a.m.–10 a.m., 11 a.m.–
3 p.m., 4:30 p.m.–7:30 p.m.,
Saturday–Sunday 9 a.m.–
10 a.m., 11 a.m.–3 p.m.,
4:30 p.m.–6:30 p.m.

Brockway Snack Bar

Food: Burger King, Ben &
Jerry's, Häagen Dazs, Sbarro,
deli sandwiches

Location: Brockway Center

Hours: Monday–Friday
7:30 a.m.–12 a.m., Saturday–
Sunday 2 p.m.–12 a.m.

Business Break

Food: Deli sandwiches

Location: School of
Management

Hours: Monday–Thursday
8 a.m.–5:30 p.m., Friday
8 a.m.–3 p.m.

Eggers Café

Food: Soups, sandwiches, hot
entrees, salad bar

Location: Eggers Hall

Hours: Monday–Thursday
8 a.m.–4 p.m., Friday 8 a.m.–
2:30 p.m.

food.com

Food: Sandwiches, soups, hot
entrees, coffee

Location: Newhouse II

(food.com, continued)

Hours: Monday–Thursday
8 a.m.–7 p.m., Friday 8 a.m.–
2:30 p.m.

Foodworks I & II

Food: Groceries, produce

Location: Robert B. Menschel
Media Center, and Dellplain
Residence Hall

Hours: Foodworks I: Monday–
Thursday 10 a.m.–10 p.m.,
Friday 10 a.m.–6 p.m.
Foodworks II: Sunday–
Thursday 5 p.m.–10 p.m.

Gallery Snack Bar

Food: Breakfast, hamburgers,
hot dogs, sandwiches, soups

Location: Marshall Hall

Hours: Monday–Friday
8 a.m.–2:30 p.m.

Goldstein Food Court

Food: Sbarro, sandwiches

Location: Goldstein Dining
Center

Hours: Monday–Friday
7:30 a.m.–12 a.m., Saturday–
Sunday 9:30 a.m.–12 a.m.

Graham Dining Hall

Food: Breakfast, lunch, dinner

Location: Graham Hall

Hours: Monday–Friday 7 a.m.
–10 a.m., 11 a.m.–3 p.m.,
4:30 p.m.–7:30 p.m.;
Saturday–Sunday 9 a.m.–
10 a.m., 11 a.m.–3 p.m.,
4:30 p.m.–6:30 p.m.

Haven Dining Hall

Food: Breakfast, lunch, dinner

Location: Haven Hall

Hours: Monday–Friday 7 a.m.
–10 a.m., 11 a.m.–3 p.m.,
4:30 p.m.–9 p.m.; Saturday–
Sunday 9 a.m.–10 a.m.,
11 a.m.–3 p.m., 4:30 p.m.–
9 p.m.

Huntington Café

Food: Entrees

Location: Huntington Hall

Hours: Monday–Friday
8 a.m.–2:30 p.m.

Jaberwocky Café

Food: Coffe, sandwiches

Location: Schine
Underground

Hours: Monday–Wednesday
7:30 a.m.–7 p.m., Thursday–
Friday 7:30 a.m.–11:30 p.m.,
Saturday 11 a.m.–11:30 p.m.,
Sunday 11 a.m.–7 p.m.

Junction Snack Bar

Food: Deli, grill

Location: Flint Hall and Day
Hall

Hours: Sunday–Thursday
7:30 p.m.–12 a.m.

Kimmel Food Court

Food: Sbarro, Dunkin'
Donuts, Häagen Dazs, Burger
King, Taco Bell, KFC, stir-fry

Location: Kimmel Dining
Center

(Kimmel, continued)

Hours: Monday–Thursday
10 a.m.–1 a.m., Friday 10 a.m.
–3 a.m., Saturday 11 a.m.–
3 a.m., Sunday 11 a.m.–
1 a.m.

Law Snack Bar

Food: Hot entrees, breakfast,
salad, deli sandwiches

Location: MacNaughton Hall

Hours: Monday–Thursday
8 a.m.–7 p.m., Friday 8 a.m.
–2:30 p.m.

Sadler Dining Hall

Food: Breakfast, lunch, dinner

Location: Sadler Hall

Hours: Monday–Friday 7 a.m.
–10 a.m., 11 a.m.–3 p.m.,
4:30 p.m.–7:30 p.m.;
Saturday–Sunday 9 a.m.–
10 a.m., 11 a.m.–3 p.m.,
4:30 p.m.–6:30 p.m.

Sadler Snack Bar

Food: Deli, grill

Location: Sadler Hall

Hours: Monday–Saturday
7 p.m.–12 a.m., Sunday
1:30 p.m.–12 a.m.

Schine Dining

Food: Sbarro, salad bar,
sandwiches, Dunkin' Donuts

Location: Schine Student
Center

Hours: Monday–Friday
7:30 a.m.–7 p.m., Saturday–
Sunday 11 a.m.–5 p.m.

Shaw Dining Hall

Food: Breakfast, lunch, dinner

Location: Shaw Hall

Hours: Monday–Friday 7 a.m.
–10 a.m., 11 a.m.–3 p.m.,
4:30 p.m.–9 p.m., Saturday–
Sunday 9 a.m.–10 a.m.,
11 a.m.–3 p.m., 4:30 p.m.–
9 p.m.

Shaw Snack Bar

Food: Sbarro, sandwiches

Location: Shaw Hall

Hours: Sunday–Thursday
8 a.m.–12 a.m., Friday–
Saturday 8 a.m.–10 p.m.

Studio Break

Food: Sandwiches, salads,
hot entrees

Location: Slocum Hall

Hours: Monday–Thursday
8 a.m.–10 p.m., Friday
8 a.m.–2:30 p.m.

Student Favorites:

Kimmel Food Court

Schine Dining

24-Hour On-Campus Eating?

No, but Kimmel is open until
3 a.m. on the weekends.

Did You Know?

The Supercard gives students the option of more food choices. This is a prepaid card on which either the students themselves or their parents put a balance at the beginning of each semester.

SU also offers a full-service restaurant on campus, called **Goldstein Faculty Center** that is not just for the University's faculty. Students are welcome at any time during its lunch hours (from 11:30 a.m.–2:30 p.m.), and they can use their Supercard dollars to pay.

Students Speak Out On...
Campus Dining

"Dining halls are okay. Sometimes, you have to pick and choose what to eat. But the food courts and the faculty dining center are both awesome."

Q "**Dining halls are horrible**. The food they serve there is completely sub-par and not of the high caliber I expected when paying $36,000 a year. The only good spot which has consistently good food is Kimmel."

Q "As a freshman, you definitely have to have a meal plan, either 14 meals or 19 meals per week. **You should go for the 14-a-week plan**, because I've never known anybody who has eaten all 19 meals on the other plan. The food here is decent, and you also get the Supercard, which can be used at the various dining centers located around campus."

Q "Food on campus isn't that bad. **They have theme nights sometimes, like Mexican night or Italian night**, so they do try to mix it up a little. To be honest, you'll get sick of dorm food eventually, but you'll always have your Supercard, which can be used at many other places."

Q "One thing about Syracuse is that **we do not have good food**! The dining halls are okay. You'll get sick of them after a while no matter what."

Q "**Dining hall food is okay**. It is probably comparable to other schools. Supercard money is great, and the Goldstein Food Court on South Campus has a great variety."

Q "The food on campus is pretty good as far as college food goes. Living off campus where you have to cook for yourself makes you appreciate those times when you could eat at the dining hall and food was cooked for you. However, **like any dining hall at any college, the food gets repetitive after a while**, and sometimes you just have to spring for a meal out on the town."

Q "If you enjoy onion rings, french fries, and chewy hamburgers, then you've come to the right place. **Most of the other food comes from Lean Cuisine as far as I've heard**. There isn't a tremendous amount of variation. Usually, I go for the food from the vegetarian section, not because I'm a vegetarian, but because the food there seems better prepared than the rest. Shaw seems consistently okay. Walking around Haven in circles only to find bad food on the other side again and again just makes me upset. Graham Dining Hall is my favorite."

Q "The dining halls on campus are not very good, unfortunately. **Certain dining centers are better than others, but as a whole, they aren't very good**. The Kimmel Dining Center, however, is very good because it consists of many large fast food franchises (Taco Bell, KFC, Burger King, Sbarro, and Dunkin' Donuts)."

Q "**I personally didn't care too much for the dining hall food**. The simple things like cereal, bread, bagels, and stuff like that are all good because you can't go wrong with any of that. You'll always find something you like, though. My favorite was the frozen yogurt."

The College Prowler Take On...
Campus Dining

The food here at SU can be summed up in one word—awful. There are, however, pros and cons, like most things at SU, and there are ways to make the most out of your dining experience. There are two types of food at SU: dining hall food and Supercard dining facilities food. The dining halls are the places on campus where you may use your meal plan; it's also where you will need the skills of Emeril Lagasse to concoct something even remotely tasty. The selection is extensive, but you will quickly get sick of making your seventh meal of the week using grilled chicken, deli meat, salad bar, and pasta. No dining hall is significantly better than the others either; although the *Daily Orange* rated Sadler and Graham dining facilities as some of the better ones, and Shaw and Haven as some of the worst. Shaw Dining Hall is also the only place on campus where Kosher food is served.

The Supercard areas, on the other hand, more than make up for the gross grub in the dining halls. These places are designated for use with cash or your prepaid Supercard. With a selection of Sbarro, Taco Bell, Burger King, KFC, Dunkin Donuts, deli sandwiches, Chinese stir-fry, and sushi, the choices are endless. Try Kimmel Dining Hall, a popular place to grab some snacks at just about any time of the day or night.

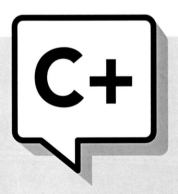

The College Prowler® Grade on Campus Dining: C+

Our grade on Campus Dining addresses the quality of both school-owned dining halls and independent on-campus restaurants as well as the price, availability, and variety of food.

Off-Campus Dining

The Lowdown On...
Off-Campus Dining

Restaurant Prowler:
Popular Places to Eat!

Acropolis Pizza House

Food: Pizza, Greek

167 Marshall Street

(315) 472-4876

Cool Features: Open after the bars on Marshall Street close, which close at 2 a.m.

Price: $6–$10 per person

Hours: Monday–Sunday
11 a.m.–12 a.m.

Aladdin's Natural Eatery

Food: All-natural, Greek

163 Marshall Street

(315) 471-4000

Cool Features: No preservatives or sulfites in any of the dishes.

Price: $7–$10 per person

Hours: Monday–Sunday
11 a.m.–11 p.m.

Alto Cinco

Food: Mexican

526 Westcott Avenue

(315) 422-6399

Cool Features: Great take-out and delivery menu.

Price: $5–$10 per person

Hours: Monday–Saturday 11 a.m–3 p.m., 5 p.m.– 11 p.m., Sunday 11 a.m.– 3 p.m., 5 p.m.–10 p.m.

Applebee's

Food: American

3189 Erie Boulevard East

(315) 445-7000

Price: $10–$25 per person

Hours: Daily 11 a.m.–12 a.m.

Baja Burrito

Food: Mexican

727 South Crouse Avenue

(315) 472-2252

Cool Features: Their burritos are made right in front of you, and you can have it made exactly the way you like.

Price: $5–$10 per person

Hours: Saturday–Wednesday 11 a.m.–8 p.m., Thursday 11 a.m.–10 p.m., Friday 11 a.m.–3 a.m.

Bennigan's Grill & Tavern

Food: American (with the "Spirit of the Irish")

2841 Erie Boulevard East

(315) 446-7575

Cool Features: Not just a restaurant, they also hold concerts and events.

Price: $10–$20 per person

Hours: Monday–Sunday 11 a.m.–12 a.m.

Cosmos Pizza & Grill

Food: Pizza, breakfast, lunch, dinner, coffee

143 Marshall Street

(315) 472-6766

Cool Features: A very laid-back, down-to-earth diner.

Price: $5–$10 per person

Hours: Monday–Friday 7 a.m.–9 p.m., Saturday 8 a.m.–2 a.m.

Delmonico's Italian Steakhouse

Food: Italian

2950 Erie Boulevard East

(315) 445-1111

Cool Features: Check out the caricatures of hundreds of famous Italians lining Delmonico's walls.

Price: $15–$25 per person

Hours: Monday–Friday 7 a.m.–10 p.m.

Dinosaur Bar-B-Que

Food: Barbeque, bar

246 West Willow Street

(315) 476-4937

Cool Features: Dinosaur Bar-B-Que's sauces are nationally acclaimed.

Price: $10–$20 per person

Hours: Monday–Thursday 11 a.m.–12 a.m., Friday–Saturday 11 a.m.–1 a.m., Sunday 12 p.m.–10 p.m.

Dorian's Gourmet Pizza & Deli

Food: Pizza, wings, subs

534 Scott Avenue

(315) 472-2697

Cool Features: 12 theme-sandwiches named after Greek gods.

Price: $10–$20 per person

Hours: Sunday–Thursday 11 a.m.–1:30 a.m., Friday–Saturday 11 a.m.–2:30 a.m.

Faegan's Café & Pub

Food: American

734 South Crouse Avenue

(315) 472-4721

Cool Features: 32 different beers on tap.

Price: $6–$10 per person

Hours: Monday–Sunday 11 a.m.–2 a.m.

Hooters

Food: American

9824 Carousel Center

(315) 466-0066

Cool Features: One of the many restaurants in Carousel Mall, including American Café and Kahunaville.

Price: $10–$20 per person

Hours: Monday–Sunday 11 a.m.–11 p.m.

King David's Restaurant

Food: Middle Eastern

129 Marshall Street

(315) 471-5000

Cool Features: The best Middle Eastern restaurant on Marshall Street.

Price: $6–$10 per person

Hours: Monday–Thursday 11 a.m.–9 p.m., Friday–Saturday 11 a.m.–10 p.m.

The Olive Garden

Food: Italian

3147 Erie Boulevard East

(315) 449-1543

Price: $10–$20 per person

Hours: Sunday–Thursday 11 a.m.–10 p.m., Friday–Saturday 11 a.m.–11 p.m.

Pastabilities

Food: Italian

311 South Franklin Street

(315) 474-1153

Cool Features: Great dining for families and couples.

Price: $10–$20 per person

Hours: Monday–Thursday 11:30 a.m.–2:30 p.m., 5 p.m.–10 p.m., Friday 11:30 a.m.–2:30 p.m., 5 p.m.–11 p.m., Saturday 5 p.m.–11 p.m., Sunday 5 p.m.–10 p.m.

The Pita Pit

Food: Mediterranean

107 Marshall Street

(315) 479-0460

Cool Features: Healthy and inexpensive dining.

Price: $5–$10 per person

Hours: Sunday–Thursday 11 a.m.–1 a.m., 11 a.m.–4:30 a.m.

Rachel's Restaurant

Food: Continental

801 University Avenue

(315) 475-3000

Cool Features: Located in the Sheraton directly next to the SU campus, this restaurant is a favorite for visiting relatives.

Price: $10–$20 per person

Hours: Daily 6:30 a.m.–10 p.m.

Scotch 'N Sirloin

Food: Steak and seafood

3687 Erie Boulevard East

(315) 446-1771

Cool Features: Award-winning wine list.

Price: $15–$25 per person

Hours: Monday–Thursday 5 p.m.–10 p.m., Friday–Saturday 5 p.m.–10:30 p.m., Sunday 10:30 a.m.–1:30 p.m. (brunch), 5 p.m.–9 p.m.

Spaghetti Warehouse

Food: Italian

689 North Clinton Street

(315) 475-1807

Cool Features: Mystery dinner theater Thursdays.

Price: $11–$15 per person

Hours: Sunday–Thursday 11 a.m.–10 p.m., Friday–Saturday 11 a.m.–11 p.m.

Tully's Good Times

Food: American

2943 Erie Boulevard East

(315) 449-9339

Cool Features: Dining/drink specials during sporting events.

Price: $8–$10 per person

Hours: Sunday–Thursday 11 a.m.–11 p.m., Friday–Saturday 11 a.m.–12:30 a.m.

Varsity Pizza

Food: Pizza

802 South Crouse Avenue

(315) 478-1235

Cool Features: Flags for SU's football opponents hang above the kitchen; when SU defeats a team, that flag is turned upside down.

Price: $5–$10 per person

Hours: Monday–Sunday
9 a.m.–9 p.m.

Student Favorites:

Acropolis Pizza House

Cosmos Pizza & Grill

Delmonico's Italian Steakhouse

Dinosaur Bar-B-Que

The Pita Pit

Tully's Good Times

Closest Grocery Stores:

Peter's Groceries, Inc.
628 South Main Street #1
(315) 458-5624

Wegman's (Fairmount)
3325 West Genesee Street
(315) 487-1581

Wegman's (Onondaga)
4722 Onondaga Boulevard
(315) 478-3313

Late-Night Snacking:

Acropolis Pizza House,
Baja Burrito

Late-Night Delivery:

Cosmos Pizza & Grill,
Dorian's Gourmet Pizza & Deli

Best Pizza:
Dorian's Gourmet Pizza & Deli

Best Breakfast:
Rachel's Restaurant

Best Wings:
Cosmos Pizza & Grill

Best Mexican:
Baja Burrito

Best Healthy:
The Pita Pit

Best Place to Take Your Parents:
Delmonico's Italian Steakhouse, Rachel's Restaurant, and Scotch 'N Sirloin

Other Places to Check Out:

Colorado Mine Co. Steakhouse

El Saha

Darwin's Restaurant & Bar

Nawab Palace

Panda West Chinese Restaurant

Samrat Indian Restaurant

Starbucks

Subway

Did You Know?

Syracuse University is a **complete Pepsi campus**. To obtain any Coca-Cola products, you must leave campus.

Students Speak Out On...
Off-Campus Dining

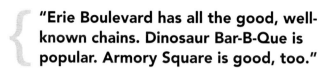

"Erie Boulevard has all the good, well-known chains. Dinosaur Bar-B-Que is popular. Armory Square is good, too."

Q "Off campus, Syracuse has some great places, and **I haven't been disappointed by any of them yet**. Nearby on Marshall Street, there are quite a few good places. Cosmos is good. I've had bad experience with Acropolis. Dinosaur Bar-B-Que is a must-visit. And if you're looking for incredible Greek pizza, Dorian's is tops. Armory Square is also good and has a great selection of pubs."

Q "**There are a few restaurants immediately off campus** that are very good. Faegan's is a pub and restaurant and offers decent meals. Delmonico's is my favorite; it's an Italian place about a mile away from campus. There's also the Dinosaur Bar-B-Que, located downtown."

Q "It's a city, so there are tons of restaurants. **The closest restaurants to campus are on Marshall Street**, which is a place you would become very familiar with. On M-Street there are two really popular pizza places (Cosmos and Acropolis), Starbucks, and a natural food place called Aladdin's (it's really good and cheap). Faegan's and Darwin's are also on Marshall Street. They're your typical bar and restaurants that serve sandwiches, salads, and pasta."

Q "I haven't been to many restaurants off campus, but **there are a few that I've enjoyed**. On Erie Boulevard, I've been to Olive Garden and an Italian steakhouse called Delmonico's. Both are very good and fit into the budget of the average college student."

Q "Syracuse offers **more dining attractions than you might expect** from a medium-sized city. Marshall Street and Erie Boulevard are the major strips of places where you catch a bite to eat."

Q "Off campus, there are a lot of places that serve good food. **Dinosaur Bar-B-Que, Colorado Steakhouse, Outback Steakhouse**, Olive Garden, Delmonico's, and Bennigan's are all great."

Q "The **restaurants are really good**. Near campus, there is Faegan's Pub, and Scotch 'N Sirloin is a steakhouse that is good, but further from campus."

Q "The restaurants off campus are **much better than the ones on campus**. Acro's, Cosmos, and Panda West are some of the good places. My favorite, however, is the Samrat Indian Restaurant and the Nawab Palace. The Indian curries they serve out here are mouth watering and awesome."

Students Speak Out On...
Off-Campus Dining

Off-campus dining can be split into two distinct categories: the restaurants within walking distance in the Marshall Street area, and restaurants within driving distance, like downtown Syracuse. Invariably, the farther away from SU you go, the better the selection of places to eat will be, but there are a few decent places that are easily accessible to freshmen. Faegan's is a bar/restaurant and one of the only locales around campus where you can enjoy a true sit-down meal. Other restaurants include: Aladdin's, Varsity, and Cosmos. Still others, like Acropolis, Baja Burrito, El Saha, and the Pita Pit are open until 2 a.m. or later on the weekends. They are very popular at those times specifically.

Stepping farther from campus, the choices are a little broader. Italian restaurants like Delmonico's Italian Steakhouse and Spaghetti Warehouse are appealing in their own ways. Delmonico's has a distinct setting, one that highlights Italian Americans in caricatures around the entire interior of the restaurant. Spaghetti Warehouse is a large restaurant that, not surprisingly, is built in an abandoned warehouse. The Warehouse is decorated with large carriages, a fair-like ambiance, and hearty meals. Try the lasagna, the house specialty. Another restaurant of note is Dinosaur Bar-B-Que, a popular locale for many SU students, as well as their families during visiting weekends. The Bar-B-Que is a biker hangout that has some of the best ribs in Syracuse. The Dinosaur Bar-B-Que sauces are famous across Central New York. Whether you choose to dine close to campus or a little further away, you are sure to satisfy your appetite.

The College Prowler® Grade on
Off-Campus Dining: B

A high Off-Campus Dining grade implies that off-campus restaurants are affordable, accessible, and worth visiting. Other factors include the variety of cuisine and the availability of alternative options (vegetarian, vegan, Kosher, etc.).

Campus Housing

The Lowdown On...
Campus Housing

Room Types:
Single, open double, split double, triple, quad, two-, three-, four-, and six-person suites

Best Dorms:
Booth, Kimmel, Marion, Watson

Worst Dorms:
Boland, Brewster, Brockway, Day, Flint

Undergrads Living on Campus:
73%

Number of Dorms:
20

Number of University-Owned Apartments:
2

→

Dormitories:

709 Comstock

Floors: 2

Total Occupancy: 35

Bathrooms: Private and shared between singles on first floor; communal on second floor

Coed: No, all women

Residents: Freshmen, sophomores, juniors, seniors

Room Types: Open double, triple

Special Features: Located near center of campus, laundry room

Boland Hall

Floors: 8

Total Occupancy: 321

Bathrooms: Communal; shared by suite

Coed: Alternating floors

Residents: Mostly freshmen

Room Types: Single, open and split double, triple, four- and six-person suites

Special Features: Garage, fitness center, laundry room, food court, study lounges, computer cluster, game room, branch of SU bookstore

Booth Hall

Floors: 8

Total Occupancy: 261

Bathrooms: Communal

Coed: Alternating rooms

Residents: Mostly underclassmen

Room Types: Single, open and split double, two- and four-person suites

Special Features: Garage, lounge/laundry room, lounges and kitchenettes on every floor

Brewster Hall

Floors: 12

Total Occupancy: 476

Bathrooms: Communal

Coed: Alternating rooms

Residents: Mostly freshmen

Room Types: Single, split double, quad, four- and six-person suites

Special Features: Garage, fitness center, laundry room, food court, study lounges, computer cluster, game room, branch of SU bookstore

Brockway

Floors: 1

Total Occupancy: 27

Bathrooms: Communal

Coed: Alternating rooms

Residents: Mostly freshmen

(Brockway, continued)

Room Types: Single, open double

Special Features: Fitness center, laundry room, food court, study lounges, computer cluster, game room, branch of SU bookstore

Day Hall

Floors: 8

Total Occupancy: 612

Bathrooms: Communal

Coed: Alternating rooms

Residents: Mostly freshmen

Room Types: Single, open and split double, quad, lofted triple

Special Features: Branch of SU bookstore, snack bar, computer cluster, laundry room, study lounge

Dellplain Hall

Floors: 8

Total Occupancy: 445

Bathrooms: Communal

Coed: Alternating rooms

Residents: Mostly underclassmen

Room Types: Single, open and split double, quad, two-, four-, and six-person suites

Special Features: Snack bar, laundry room, TV lounges with microwaves on each floor

Flint Hall

Floors: 4

Total Occupancy: 537

Bathrooms: Communal

Coed: Alternating rooms

Residents: Mostly freshmen

Room Types: Single, open double, lofted triple

Special Features: Branch of SU bookstore, snack bar, computer cluster, laundry room, study lounge

Haven Hall

Floors: 11

Total Occupancy: 373

Bathrooms: Communal

Coed: Alternating floors (floors 1–3); alternating rooms (floors 4–11)

Residents: Mostly underclassmen

Room Types: Single, open and split double, one-, two-, and four-person suites

Special Features: Conference room, meeting room, study lounge, pool table, laundry room, adjoining dining center, TV lounges with microwaves on each floor

International Living Center (ILC)

Floors: 3

Total Occupancy: 40

Bathrooms: Communal

Coed: Alternating floors

(ILC, continued)

Residents: Freshman, sopomore, junior, senior (both International and domestic students)

Room Types: Single, open double, triple

Special Features: A "Learning Community," designed to foster deeper cultural understanding

Kimmel Hall

Floors: 3

Total Occupancy: 121

Bathrooms: Communal

Coed: Alternating floors

Residents: Mostly underclassmen

Room Types: Open double, lofted triple

Special Features: Fitness center, laundry room, computer cluster, TV lounge

Lawrinson Hall

Floors: 21

Total Occupancy: 565

Bathrooms: Communal

Coed: Alternating Floor

Residents: Mostly freshmen

Room Types: Single, split double, triple

Special Features: Branch of SU bookstore, computer cluster, laundry room, storage room and TV lounge with microwaves on each floor

Marion Hall

Floors: 3

Total Occupancy: 153

Bathrooms: Communal

Coed: Alternating rooms

Residents: Mostly underclassmen

Special Features: Fitness center, laundry room, computer cluster, TV lounge, kitchenette

Sadler Hall

Floors: 8

Total Occupancy: 489

Bathrooms: Communal; some private on first floor

Coed: Alternating wings

Residents: Mostly freshmen

Room Types: Single, open and split double, triple, lofted triple, four- and six-person suites

Special Features: TV lounge with microwave, game room, snack bar, laundry room, study lounges, dining center

Shaw Hall

Floors: 5, plus ground floor

Total Occupancy: 451

Bathrooms: Communal

Coed: Alternating wings (floors G–2); alternating rooms (floors 3–5)

Residents: Mostly underclassmen

(Shaw Hall, continued)

Room Types: Single, open and split double, triple

Special Features: Classrooms, art room, snack bar, computer cluster, laundry room, TV lounge, dining center, multipurpose room

Sheraton

Floors: 1 (fourth floor of SU-adjacent Sheraton Inn)

Total Occupancy: 32

Bathrooms: Private

Coed: Alternating rooms

Residents: Students in need of temporary housing or greater privacy

Room Types: Open double

Special Features: Laundry room, housekeeping services, near center of campus

Skyhalls I, II, and III

Floors: 3 each

Total Occupancy: 60 each in Skyhalls I and II; 117 in Skyhall III

Bathrooms: Communal

Coed: Alternating rooms

Residents: Mostly underclassmen

Room Types: Large singles in Skyhalls I and II, open doubles in Skyhall III

Special Features: Study lounge and two kitchens on each floor

Skytop Apartments

Floors: 90 two-story townhouses

Total Occupancy: 1,900

Bathrooms: Private

Coed: Yes

Residents: Upperclassmen

Room Types: Two- and three-bedroom apartments

Special Features: Ski lodge, multipurpose center, student center, ice skating pavillion

Slocum Heights

Floors: 35 two-story buildings

Total Occupancy: 250

Bathrooms: Private

Coed: Yes

Residents: Families and grad students

Room Types: One- and two-bedroom apartments

Special Features: Specialty apartment-style housing

Walnut Hall

Floors: 4

Total Occupancy: 46

Bathrooms: Communal

Coed: Alternating floors

Residents: Upperclassmen

Room Types: Large single, open double, large open double

Special Features: TV lounge, meeting room, study lounge, kitchen, dining room

Washington Arms

Floors: 5

Total Occupancy: 62

Bathrooms: Private; shared by suite

Coed: Alternating rooms/ suites

Residents: Upperclassmen

Room Types: Open double, two- and three-person suites

Special Features: TV lounge, laundry room, study lounge, rec room, kitchenettes on each floor

Watson Hall

Floors: 4

Total Occupancy: 446

Bathrooms: Communal; some shared by suite

Coed: Alternating rooms

Residents: Upperclassmen

(Watson Hall, continued)

Room Types: Single, open double, two-, three-, four-, and six-person suites, three- and four-person townhouse suites

Special Features: Study room, campus grocery, snack bar, theater complex, laundry room, 24-hour study room, game room (with pool and Ping-Pong tables)

Housing Offered:

Singles: 14%

Doubles: 51%

Triples/Suites: 7%

Apartments: 28%

Bed Type

Twin extra-long

Cleaning Service?

Yes, maintenance staff cleans every day. Also, you can submit a maintenance/repair request to FIXit, the housing maintenance staff, at (315) 443-4948.

What You Get

Each student receives a bed, desk, Ethernet connection, and a cable connection.

Did You Know?

The newest dorms on campus are Brewster and Boland, which were built in 1968. The oldest dorm is Shaw Hall, which was built in 1952. Many of the dorms have been renovated since then.

Students Speak Out On...
Campus Housing

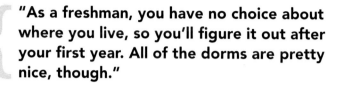

"As a freshman, you have no choice about where you live, so you'll figure it out after your first year. All of the dorms are pretty nice, though."

Q "When I was a freshman, **the Mount seemed like the most fun**. It might have been a hike to get there, but there was always something going on. Aside from the sometimes-bigger rooms at Lawrinson, Sadler, and Brewster/Boland, they really aren't worth the eight- to fifteen-minute walk to main campus, especially in blizzards. Watson has the biggest, nicest rooms, but people are cliquey there."

Q "Dorms are not like hotels, but **they are enough to keep you warm and safe**."

Q "SU has a dorm room style known as a split double, which doesn't seem to be common among other universities as far as I know. It's a dorm room with a partition in the middle giving each roommate their own private space. The suites in Haven and Booth are some of the best suites on North Campus. **All the dorms at SU have wall-to-wall carpeting**. The dorms that students try to stay away from are Brewster/Boland because they seem to have the worst location on campus. For the most part, however, all of the dorm rooms at SU are clean and have a lot of space."

Q "Some dorms are nice, some aren't. **Aim to get into the freshman dorms like Day or Flint**, although if you end up living there, you'll probably encounter many superficial snobs. Haven is the nicest dorm on campus."

Q "**All the facilities are adequate**; however, if you get Watson, Booth, or Dellplain, you've lucked out."

Q "In comparison to other schools that I've seen, **the dorms are pretty nice**. A lot of freshmen live in Flint and Day, which are newer. They are kind of set back from campus up on a hill, but they are still close to everything. Other dorms for freshmen are Lawrinson, Sadler, Brewster, and Boland. I've never heard of anyone complain about them. Most people love their dorms."

Q "Dorms are good, but **you definitely should get a split double**. Avoid the Mount and Brewster/Boland."

Q "Stay away from the Brewster and Boland dorms. **Kimmel is the best dorm to live in**."

Q "Overall, **the dorms are awesome**. Location is the problem. Brewster/Boland is really far away from everything, and Flint and Day (on the Mount) require walking up and down over a hundred steps to get to campus."

The College Prowler Take On...
Campus Housing

All dorms have their perks, and most dorms have their downfalls. The students in Day and Flint Halls live on Mount Olympus, literally and figuratively, but you must field over 100 stairs to get to the top. Brewster and Boland dorms are the farthest away from campus. That fact allows them to get away with being the only dorms with a Taco Bell in the basement and their own library. Sadler and Lawrinson Halls are at the bottom corner of campus where nothing social ever happens, except of course if you want to meet up at the Carrier Dome that is in arm's reach from the dorms.

Then there are the dorms with which students have no major qualms. These dorms include Kimmel, Marion, Shaw, Booth, Dellplain, Haven, and Watson Halls. With the exception of Shaw, all these dorms primarily house upperclassmen. They also are located closer to the main campus, as well as Marshall Street and Comstock and Walnut Avenues—prime party locations. If you end up with one of these dorms, consider yourself extremely lucky. Finally, although you have no say whether you end up in an open or split double, cross your fingers for the split. This way, if you and your roommate clash in any way, you have some separation between you. This split double design is not offered at many universities, and it is a welcome addition to SU.

The College Prowler® Grade on

Campus Housing: B-

A high Campus Housing grade indicates that dorms are clean, well-maintained, and spacious. Other determining factors include variety of dorms, proximity to classes, and social atmosphere.

Off-Campus Housing

The Lowdown On...
Off-Campus Housing

Undergrads in Off-Campus Housing:

27%

Average Rent for:
1BR Apt.: $450/month
2BR Apt.: $575/month
3BR Apt.: $700/month

Best Time to Look for a Place:
Early September, a year in advance

Popular Places:

Comstock Avenue

Euclid Avenue

For Assistance Contact:

Office of Off-Campus Student Services

(315) 443-5489

ocsserv@syr.edu

Orange Housing
www.orangehousing.com

Students Speak Out On...
Off-Campus Housing

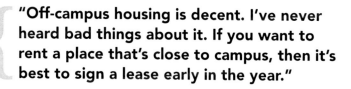

"Off-campus housing is decent. I've never heard bad things about it. If you want to rent a place that's close to campus, then it's best to sign a lease early in the year."

Q "Student at SU are **not permitted to live off campus until their junior year**. When this time comes, many students rush to find the nicest and closest house or apartment to campus. Many students choose to live on South Campus because the apartments are large and tend to be readily available upon request. Living off campus, in my opinion, is worth it because it allows students to have an opportunity to live on their own; it also tends to be cheaper than living on North and South Campus."

Q "For the price and the space you gain, **living off campus is very worth it**. Next year, three of my friends and I are living 12 minutes off campus and are paying $260 a month each to live in a big house. That's over $300 less than the cost of living in a dorm."

Q "You have to stay on campus for two years, but when the time comes and you want to move off campus, **there will be several advertisements in the newspaper** to get you started with you search."

Q "**There are shuttle buses that run every 15 minutes** until about 3 a.m. My house is one of the farthest from campus on the route, and it's still only about a mile away."

Q "Junior year is the best time to move off campus. **You're more likely to find a place**, and when you do, you'll find that they are so much cheaper than on-campus rooms."

Q "**Off-campus housing is very convenient**. During junior and senior year, most people live off campus. In most ways, it is definitely worth it."

Q "Everyone has a two-year housing contract. Girls often will move into their sorority houses. South Campus also offers an apartment-style feeling. **There's freedom there, but it is pretty far from campus**."

Q "**Off-campus housing usually proves amenable to students's needs**. The campus is surrounded by several inexpensive residential neighborhoods. There are tons of houses and apartments that you can rent for very little money."

Q "Off-campus housing is **never convenient without a car of your own**. Yes, buses are constantly available and are made to be as convenient as possible, but it can be annoying and a chore. Most people move off campus their junior year. It is definitely worth the move financially. You will be saving your parents over $1,500 in most cases. My opinion is that it is definitely worth it."

The College Prowler Take On...
Off-Campus Housing

There is a broad selection when choosing an off-campus house. Most students find it both appealing and fairly easy to move into an off-campus house or apartment in their junior year. One of the main appeals is simply a matter of economics—living off campus costs less than living in the dorms. Also, most off-campus locations are close to campus (within a 20-minute walk), and you are afforded a little more freedom since there are no RAs or Public Safety officers to bother you. The process can be a bit lengthy, since there are many realtors and many locations to choose from. Make sure you start your search about a year in advance.

A good alternative to off-campus housing are the SU-owned apartment complexes in South Campus, which require a five-minute drive or bus ride to get to. South, as it is known, is a good option for someone to live outside of the dorms but not completely on their own. South is usually a popular choice for sophomores. Although technically considered on-campus housing, the South Campus apartments give a good "partially off-campus" feel. Students seem to enjoy the apartment-style living option because it is a good transition point between dormitory life and being completely on your own. However, many students choose to live entirely on their own, and they enjoy it just fine—except for having to walk everywhere. If you do decide to move off campus, a car is an investment you should take into serious consideration.

The College Prowler® Grade on

Off-Campus Housing: A-

A high grade in Off-Campus Housing indicates that apartments are of high quality, close to campus, affordable, and easy to secure.

Diversity

The Lowdown On...
Diversity

Native American:
0%

White:
81%

Asian American:
5%

International:
3%

African American:
6%

Unknown:
1%

Hispanic:
4%

Out-of-State:
55%

Political Activity

There are a bunch of political groups on campus. They tend to be more prevalent on campus during times of political distress in the world beyond SU. Due to the recent events in the U.S., the political scene has dramatically increased in visibility.

Gay Pride

You won't find many acts of intolerance against homosexuals at SU. The city of Syracuse has a fairly active gay community, both politically and socially, as there are many clubs aimed towards gays in the area. At SU, there is a Pride Union, as well as a LGBT (Lesbian, Gay, Bisexual and Transgender) resource center on campus.

Most Popular Religions

There is a large variety when it comes to religion, as well. Although SU probably has more Jewish students than most colleges, the percentage is not overwhelming one way or the other. There are many churches within walking distance of the campus, as well as a few temples and one mosque. The new Winnick Hillel Center has boosted interest in the Jewish organization.

Economic Status

Although students come from many different economic and social backgrounds, the majority of students at SU fall either in the middle- or upper-middle-class category. Being a private school, and an expensive one at that, it leads to this distinction. Interaction between castes, however, has never been an issue.

Minority Clubs

SU has an abundance of clubs that cater to very specific groups. Such clubs as the African Students Union, Asian Students in America, Association of International Students, and Caribbean Students Association are just some of the many clubs aimed at minorities. However, there are also clubs like the Multiracial Experience and Students Advocating Multicultural Equality that bring cultures and races together.

Students Speak Out On...
Diversity

> "Syracuse is supposed to be the seventh most diverse campus in the country. The numbers seem to support that, I guess, but most of the kids seem to come from New York and New Jersey."

Q "The campus is very diverse, **the largest minority groups being African Americans and Hispanics**, which make up about 10 percent of the campus. It is also about 14 percent Jewish, so that is kind of weird for people who didn't grow up in that kind of environment. We have a huge problem with intermingling among the ethnic groups. Students pretty much keep to themselves."

Q "In numbers, SU is very diverse; however, **there isn't much mingling between groups**."

Q "The campus is extremely diverse. That's one of the nice things about going to a university: you will meet so many people of different races, religions, and personalities. **They come from all over the world**."

Q "**They advertise the school to be much more diverse than it really is**. Unless diversity means that some people come from Connecticut and some come from New Jersey, they really shouldn't keep bragging about it."

Q "One of the main ideals of the Syracuse University Compact (campus-wide mission statement) is to promote a diverse atmosphere. **Syracuse University promotes diversity**, however, most of the people you see on campus are Caucasian."

Q "**They like to brag about SU being diverse**, and to a certain extent, I think it is. There are a lot of different ethnic groups represented on campus."

Q "The diversity on campus is very rich. In SU, you will find people that differ widely in terms of values, ethics, morality, countries, and family background. My experience with diversity in school has been very good, as **I got the opportunity to work in teams with really diverse backgrounds**."

Q "One of the most valuable things I have learned out here is to **maximize the benefits of diversity**. We all have so much to learn from each other."

The College Prowler Take On...
Diversity

SU, like most colleges, likes to brag about having a culturally-diverse student body. Although Syracuse may not be the most diverse campus around, there are a significant number of minority students here. That said, pure numbers and statistics do not determine the true diversity level on a college campus; intermingling between cultures is what's important. However, Syracuse, like many other "diverse" universities, shows a distinct lack of social interaction between people of different backgrounds. Whether it is in the student center or in the extracurricular activities students chose to participate in, the separation is evident, despite the University's best efforts to promote cultural unity. On the other hand, though, students of different economic backgrounds mesh together here quite well.

There is, however, a great number or clubs and organizations that cater to minority students. Black and Latino fraternities are an influential force in bringing dances and speakers to SU. Places like the LGBT (Lesbian, Gay, Bisexual, and Transgender) Resource Center and the Winnick Hillel Center are key elements of the SU community, and they are welcome to everyone, not just people that fit their respective group interests. Also, majors like Middle Eastern, Native American, African American, and Latino American studies are seeing a rise in student interest.

B

The College Prowler® Grade on
Diversity: B

A high grade in Diversity indicates that ethnic minorities and international students have a notable presence on campus and that students of different economic backgrounds, religious beliefs, and sexual preferences are well represented.

Guys & Girls

The Lowdown On...
Guys & Girls

Men Undergrads:
42%

Women Undergrads:
58%

Birth Control Available?

Only condoms are avilable on campus.

Social Scene

Most students go out at least once a week. Often, students will congregate with friends for a pre-game that usually includes only their closest friends. As the night progresses (around 10 p.m.), students will go out to the bars, frats, house parties, or simply hang out in the dorm on the weekends.

Hookups or Relationships?

There is not a great deal of dating per se, but there are quite a few people in long-term, exclusive relationships and a lot of friends-with-benefits. Especially for freshmen, both guys and girls usually want to experience their first year in college without the burden of commitment. That is, of course, unless the individual comes into their freshman year with a boyfriend or girlfriend from home, which is the case quite often. These long-distance relationships rarely last more than a few months in the sexually-charged atmosphere of SU. Still, many couples end up in committed, long-term relationships even after they leave Syracuse.

Best Place to Meet Guys/Girls

For some students, the best place to meet is simply in the library—a place where many attractive guys and girls gather to get some studying in before the weekend begins. Other students meet significant others at the bars or the frat parties around campus. These can be very good spots to hook up, but it's rarely the best method for finding a long-term relationship. The best place to make contacts and meet hotties is probably (and surprisingly) in class. Sure, it might not be the best setting for a romantic rendezvous, but since so much time is spent in the classrooms of SU, there is no better way to make small talk, get numbers, and get the ball rolling for something greater. Also, it doesn't hurt that many classes assign projects where you need to work with a partner, almost always of your own selection.

Dress Code

There is no set dress code at SU, but it's pretty safe to say that besides the first few weeks of school and the last few weeks of school, there will be very little time to spend in mini-skirts, shorts, and tank-tops walking around the campus. This makes it imperative to break out the true summer clothes whenever there is an indoors event—like going to the gym or going to bars and frats. Some students on campus dress in the trendiest outfits available, while others prefer more laid-back sweatpants and sweatshirts. There is a very eclectic mix of style at SU.

Did You Know?

Top Places to Find Hotties:

1. Bars—check out Darwin's or Chuck's.
2. Frats—during parties, check out Deke, Sammy, Sigma Nu, and SAE.
3. Archbold Gymnasium

Top Places to Hook Up:

1. His room
2. Her room
3. Frat party (Although, it is sometimes considered taboo to hook up in front of a large group of people.)
4. Bars
5. On a date

Students Speak Out On...
Guys & Girls

"It's impossible to describe all the guys and girls. So many different people go here. They're all unique. Some are hot, some not so much."

"The guys here tend to be better looking than the girls. It depends on who you meet, of course, but some SU women can be extremely snobby, extremely rude, very wealthy, and drive $50,000 cars."

"SU has many good-looking women. It's interesting because most of the women at SU are very attractive, and it is rare to find a woman that is below the standards of most men, although they do exist."

"The guys here are hot, but sometimes, I think that they are all the same. I haven't met a guy whom I've felt to be truly genuine in three years. But they are hot and nice to look at. The girls are the same; not too many real winners, but then again, I know tons of people that have met and dated people here for years, and some have even gotten married."

"Some Syracuse guys are hot, but this campus is very diverse, so you can find just about whatever type of guy you're looking for. I honestly don't look at the guys that much, but there are some true studs around."

"Girls are so hot here!"

Q "I haven't found my dream guy yet, but **there are plenty of great-looking ones here**."

Q "Well, honestly, this should not be a determining factor in your choice of a college that's right for you. But **the guys and girls here are pretty attractive**. I think it's the whole Greek thing that attracts those people."

Q "Most of the guys I know are good people, but like all places in the world, there is that huge group of 'better-off-dead' types. As for the girls, there is a huge majority of hotness, but **there are tons of airheads**."

The College Prowler Take On...
Guys & Girls

SU is notorious for its good-looking guys and girls, and it's not just a stereotype. The main downfall of having so many attractive people at SU is that the weather causes their good looks to go to waste, buried beneath layers of clothing. It's easy to meet people at Syracuse mainly due to its slightly larger than average student population. This way, you will always be meeting new people while still being able to keep in touch with the objects of last week's affection. Some girls, however, tend to think there are far more guys looking for a casual hookups than long-term relationships.

On the personality scale, however, SU is home to a host of different character traits. Students seem to think that a significant number of egotistical, rich students (both males and females) attend this university. Still, that number is balanced easily by the broad range of other personalities on campus. Here, you can find not just the ostentatious type; you'll find some hippie-type groups, potheads, intellectuals, overachievers, drunks, and athletes. Sound like high school? Well, maybe, but there is far more intermingling between personality types and financial backgrounds. It's relatively close quarters at SU, so this is cause for some unity. Also, you'll meet many good-looking people that span every group and clique in your four years here.

The College Prowler® Grade on

Guys: B+

A high grade for Guys indicates that the male population on campus is attractive, smart, friendly, and engaging, and that the school has a decent ratio of guys to girls.

The College Prowler® Grade on

Girls: A-

A high grade for Girls not only implies that the women on campus are attractive, smart, friendly, and engaging, but also that there is a fair ratio of girls to guys.

Athletics

The Lowdown On...
Athletics

Athletic Division:
Division I

Conference:
Big East

School Mascot:
Otto the Orange

**Males Playing
Varsity Sports:**
320 (6%)

**Females Playing
Varsity Sports:**
270 (4%)

→

Men's Varsity Sports:

Basketball
Crew
Cross-Country
Football
Lacrosse
Soccer
Swimming & Diving
Track & Field

Women's Varsity Sports:

Basketball
Cross-Country
Field Hockey
Lacrosse
Rowing
Softball
Soccer
Swimming & Diving
Tennis
Volleyball
Track & Field

Club Sports:

Aikido
Badminton
Ballroom Dance
Baseball
Bowling
Breakdance
Cricket
Curling
Cycling

(Club Sports, continued)

Dance Works
Equestrian
Fencing
Field Hockey
Figure Skating
Golf
Gymnastics
Ice Hockey
Lacrosse
Martial Arts
Paintball
Roller Hockey
Rugby

Intramurals:

Basketball
Broomball
Cricket
Flag Football
Floor Hockey
Racquetball
Shotokan
Ski Racing
Soccer
Softball
Table Tennis
Tennis
Triathlon
Ultimate Frisbee
Volleyball
Wallyball

Athletic Fields

Carrier Dome, Hendricks Field, Manley Field House, Skytop Field, Tennity Ice Pavilion, and Women's Building Field

Getting Tickets

It is relatively easy to get tickets at SU. For football, basketball, and lacrosse, there are season ticket packages available for students to pre-order before the year begins. For individual game tickets, the only tough ones to get are for football and men's basketball; otherwise, as long as you buy them a little in advance, they should be easy to get. All students sit in the same section in the Carrier Dome, so make sure you go early to get a nice seat to cheer with your friends. You can buy tickets online at *http://carrierdome.syr.edu*.

Most Popular Sports

Men's basketball, football, and lacrosse

Overlooked Teams

Men's hockey

Best Place to Take a Walk

Manley Field House track, the Quad

Gyms/Facilities

Archbold Gymnasium, Drumlin's Tennis Club and Golf Course (a 5-minute drive from the SU campus), Flanigan Gymnasium, and Tennity Ice Pavilion.

Students Speak Out On...
Athletics

{ ”Sports at Syracuse are huge, as one might expect of a Division I school. They tend to bring a lot of money to the school. You'll definitely enjoy watching them, and they are a huge part of campus life.”

Q "**Varsity sports are pretty big here**. It's usually not a problem getting tickets to football, basketball, and lacrosse games, so I would recommend going to some games because they can be a lot of fun. Intramural sports are fun, too, and we have just about every club you could imagine, as well.”

Q "Basketball is very big. **Football is semi-popular**. There are lots of club teams that sort of serve as JV teams.”

Q "In football and basketball, **we have some of the best teams in the NCAA**, and a lot of people come to school because of that. Intramural sports are great here, and I've taken part in both an indoor soccer league and a broomball league. [My department also has] basketball tournaments.”

Q "**There are three big varsity sports at SU: men's football, basketball, and lacrosse**. They are all very popular; however, basketball draws the most excitement at the Dome in my opinion. With a national championship under the team's belt, there are many expectations to succeed again. The intramural sports at SU are popular, as well; however, I've only participated in intramural football.”

Q "**Varsity sports are huge**! Have you ever seen a Syracuse football game or basketball game on TV? Being in the Carrier Dome is crazy! The games are totally off-the-wall, and the Dome gets so loud! If you're into indoor soccer, there are great games to go to if you want to see some of that. We were also the national champions in men's lacrosse, and their games are pretty crazy, too."

Q "Our football and basketball games are always quite an event—**they're really, really fun to attend**. I would recommend going. Syracuse also has some really nice facilities for intramural sports."

Q "**This is a big sports school**. Basketball, football, and lacrosse are huge. Not only do the school and students have high levels of support, you realize that so does the town of Syracuse. During your years, you will see many 'townies' at the SU games."

Q "This is a huge sports school, especially for football and basketball. **We have a really big intramural program, as well**."

The College Prowler Take On...
Athletics

Sports in Syracuse (as a city) are huge. Syracuse is an Orange town through and through, and everywhere you go you will find support for the Orange. On the SU campus, the sentiment is not as pronounced. In the two major sports (football and basketball), SU students differ in their fanaticism. Football can draw some hardcore fans, and as most sports teams, some fair-weather fans. Basketball, however, brings out a unified, campus-wide pride. The successful 2002–2003 season might have had something to do with the boost in supportive school spirit for the basketball team. SU students just can't get enough of the basketball team. One main reason students love varsity sports is the Carrier Dome—the setting for all football, men's basketball, and men's lacrosse home games. The Dome is great for football, especially when it's snowing outside, as well as basketball. The best part about the Dome is its location—right in the middle of the SU campus.

Intramural sports are fairly popular at SU. Flag football and basketball are the big draws, and they can get competitive—unfortunately, maybe a little too competitive. The rules are very strictly enforced, which is why pick-up games seem to be the better option for most of the students on the SU campus.

The College Prowler® Grade on
Athletics: A+

A high grade in Athletics indicates that students have school spirit, that sports programs are respected, that games are well-attended, and that intramurals are a prominent part of student life.

Nightlife

The Lowdown On...
Nightlife

Club and Bar Prowler:
Popular Nightlife Spots!

Club Crawler:

The club scene in Syracuse is not very prominent. For one, there are really no clubs close to the campus; also, students seem to prefer bars over clubs in general.

Club 950

950 Spencer Street

(315) 425-1450

A local lesbian dance club featuring a funky atmosphere with eye-catching artwork, pop and dance music, weekly karaoke, drag king shows (that's kings, not queens), and great food. Closed Mondays and Tuesdays.

➜

The Country Club

Erie Boulevard East at Bridge Street, Dewitt, NY

(315) 445-2527

One of the most celebrated night spots in upstate NY, the Country Club has a chic clientele, a packed dancefloor, plush Romanesque architecture, and DJs spinning mostly rock, pop, and house—though on Fridays, it becomes a massive Southern hoedown with country music and two-stepping all night long. Open to 18 and over.

Bar Prowler:

The bar scene on campus can be split into two categories: those within walking distance, and those that require vehicular transportation. Subsequently, the bars in Armory Square and downtown Syracuse cater to an older crowd, while the bars on the SU hill feature almost entirely SU students, and even some underclassmen.

SU Hill:
Chuck's Café & Bar

727 South Crouse Avenue

(315) 477-1544

As "Hungry Charlie's," this bar was once notorious for its loose underage drinking policies, but they closed down voluntarily and set up shop in the guise of an "espresso bar." Don't let that fool you, though; this is still a good bar with good music and drink specials—but expect to be carded.

Darwin's Restaurant & Bar

701 South Crouse Avenue

(315) 472-1901

A good mix of American continental dining and bar/nightclub, Darwin's has live blues performances, DJs on the weekends, a big screen TV, and a great view of SU campus, as well as great all-you-can-eat lunch buffet.

Faegan's Café & Pub

734 South Crouse Avenue

(315) 472-4721

In addition to it's laid-back atmosphere and weekly live jazz and blues performances, Faegan's boasts 32 different beers on tap, including domestics, imports, and microbrews. A popular favorite among beer lovers.

Lucy's Retired Surfers

721 South Crouse Avenue

(315) 476-9990

The So-Cal theme might feel a bit out of place in Syracuse, but this is still a fun bar where the DJs spin surf music as well as the typical top-40 fare, and the Corona flows like water. You can also get a spot in the VIP room for $5, as well.

Maggie's Tavern

720 University Avenue

(315) 424-1325

Maggie's makes it a point to cater to the Greek crowd, and the walls are decorated with fraternity and sorority memorabilia. They host several Greek events, as well.

Downtown Syracuse/ Armory Square:
Blue Tusk

165 Walton Street

(315) 472-1934

This is a very classy beer-bar and a staple of the Syracuse bar scene. Blue Tusk features nearly 70 varieties of beer on tap from all over the world, all served in 20 ounce "imperial" pints. Expensive, yes, but worth the experience.

Daniel Jack's Entertainment Restaurant

218 Walton Street

(315) 475-8357

Thursday night is Trivia Night, where a $50 bar tab prize. Also features a happy hour and musical entertainment.

Limerick Pub

134 Walton Street

(315) 475-1819

This is a traditional Irish pub with good sandwiches, pool tables, and low-density crowds.

PJ Dorsey's Pub & Grill

116 Walton Street

(315) 478-3023

A fun bar with a good crowd and Irish music. It's also connected to the acclaimed PJ Dorsey's Steakhouse, so you can stop in there for some upscale dining before hitting the bar—don't expect to eat cheaply, though.

Bars Close At:

2 a.m.

Cheapest Place to Get a Drink:

Happy hour at Chuck's Cafe & Bar or Armory Square

Primary Areas with Nightlife:

Marshall Street (especially good for those without a car), and Armory Square around Walton and West Fayette Street

Other Places to Check Out:

Blue Tusk

Favorite Drinking Games:

Beirut/Beer Pong

Circle of Death

Flip Cup

Power Hour

Cardinal Puff

Student Favorites:

Chuck's Cafe & Bar

Darwin's Restaurant & Bar

Useful Resources for Nightlife:

The Daily Orange

The Syracuse New-Times

The Syracuse Post-Standard

What to Do if You're Not 21

There are many great coffee shops and venues in the SU area. Check out Happy Ending on South Clinton Street or the Westcott Community Center on Euclid Avenue to hear live music on the weekends. Also, on Friday nights until around 8 p.m., anyone over 18 can head to Chuck's on Marshall Street and either eat or hang out with their 21-and-over friends.

Frats

See the Greek section!

Students Speak Out On...
Nightlife

"There are a lot of bars on Marshall Street, but a lot of them are annoying places to go. The best place over there is either Darwin's or Faegan's."

Q "The party scene on campus is **popular for freshmen** who can go to tons of house parties for cheap. They pretty much stop during the winter, though. We have a ton of bars to choose from both on Marshall Street and in Armory Square that are all really good."

Q "The parties on campus are fun as a freshman. After a year of Greek parties, **it becomes generic and banal**. As a freshman, live it up at frat parties, but for every year after that, I recommend the bar scene. The good bars are Darwin's, Chuck's, and Lucy's."

Q "The **Greek life at SU is fun** and continues to be the main place to party as a freshman or sophomore. The bar scene off campus tends to be the place to party for many upperclassmen. Chuck's draws a lot of attention from the student body. I haven't been to any clubs off campus."

Q "In the '90s, **Syracuse used to have a great reputation as a party school**, and now in the 21st century, parties are still kicking. Be sure you make good friends with your RA before you throw a room party, or at least don't have them when he/she's on the floor. I haven't been to any bars or clubs."

Q "Bars are great, but there is not really a club scene. **Frat parties are okay, but they can get crowded**. There are a few good theme parties, though."

Q "**The bars around campus are usually invaded by sorority girls and fraternity boys**. If you're not into that scene, then the bars suck. In Armory Square, the bars are much better—less like high school."

Q "Darwin's, Faegan's, Lucy's, and Maggie's are the places to be. **There are also some good bars downtown** like PJ Dorsey's, Limerick's, Blue Tusk, and other such places."

Q "I just turned 21, so I haven't really had much experience with the bars on campus, but from what I have experienced, I can tell you that they are really quite fun. **You've just got to try them all out and see which ones you really like**."

The College Prowler Take On...
Academics

Partying at Syracuse has a split personality—some days are great and some are bad. That swing from good to bad can be very drastic and sudden, but for the casual partier, SU will more than suffice. Most weekends, there will be at least one frat party (where the majority of parties occur) and a few house parties. Those who like 100–200 people jammed in a basement waiting in line for the keg should head towards Frat Row on Comstock Avenue. It might not sound appealing, but it's a perfect setting for freshmen. You can meet new people and bond with the ones you met a few weeks before.

Of course, there will be weekends where absolutely nothing is happening. During these weeks, many students choose to patronize the bars. You have to find the bar that's right for you, but be careful: as part of Operation Prevent, Syracuse cops have been cracking down hard on underage drinkers, including conducting bar raids. This means two things: the bouncers will be more strict when looking at IDs, and there always will be a fear that the bar where you are pounding kamikazes will get raided. In April 2004, Konrad's, one of the more notorious bars for underage drinking, was shut down after too many raids. Use extreme caution when going out to the bars underage. On the weekends, the nightlife is evident in the dorms, as well, and if you want to do work, you should head to a computer cluster or to the library to avoid the debauchery. If you are partying in the dorms, make sure you have an RA who can tolerate some noise.

The College Prowler® Grade on

Nightlife: B-

A high grade in Nightlife indicates that there are many bars and clubs in the area that are easily accessible and affordable. Other determining factors include the number of options for the under-21 crowd and the prevalence of house parties.

Greek Life

The Lowdown On...
Greek Life

**Number of
Fraternities:**
22

**Undergrad Men
in Fraternities:**
19%

**Number of
Sororities:**
13

**Undergrad Women
in Sororities:**
20%

→

Fraternities:

Acacia
Alpha Chi Rho
Alpha Epsilon Pi
Alpha Tau Omega
Delta Chi
Delta Kappa Epsilon
Delta Tau Delta
Kappa Delta Rho
Phi Gamma Delta
Phi Kappa Psi
Phi Kappa Theta
Pi Kappa Alpha
Psi Psi
Psi Upsilon
Sigma Alpha Epsilon
Sigma Alpha Mu
Sigma Nu
Sigma Phi Epsilon
Tau Kappa Epsilon
Theta Chi
Zeta Beta Tau
Zeta Psi

Sororities:

Alpha Chi Omega
Alpha Epsilon Phi
Alpha Gamma Delta
Alpha Phi
Alpha Xi Delta
Delta Delta Delta
Delta Gamma
Gamma Phi Beta
Kappa Alpha Theta
Kappa Kappa Gamma
Phi Beta Phi
Phi Sigma Sigma
Sigma Delta Tau

Other Greek Organizations:

Interfraternity Council
Latino Greek Council
Multicultural Greek Council
National Pan-Hellenic Council
Pan-Hellenic Council

Multicultural Colonies:

Lambda Pi Chi
Omerga Phi Beta
Sigma Iota Alpha
Phi Iota Alpha

Did You Know?

Although many fraternities hold parties sometime during the semester, **no sorority can throw a party**. That means two things: one, the sorority houses are usually extremely well-kept and clean—as opposed to the frats—and two, the houses are also much more exclusive, as only those involved in the sorority are generally allowed to hang out there.

Students Speak Out On...
Greek Life

{ **"Sometimes it may seem that Greek life dominates the social scene, but since it's such a big school, there are plenty of ways to avoid it if you're not into it."**

Q "I'm not Greek, but a lot of my friends are. **It does somewhat control the social scene**, as I think that about 40 percent of the campus is Greek. It's very cliquey and superficial, but a lot of fun, too. I think you'd have to rush so that you could find out more about it during that process."

Q "**Greek life only will dominate school for you if you are involved in it**. If you aren't, you hardly notice it."

Q "**Greek life kind of has its own thing going on**. They take over things like homecoming and definitely throw a lot of parties, but it's totally your call if you go that route. There are people who do love it and spend a lot of their time with their brothers or sisters and the people who don't choose to go Greek also have a great time, too."

Q "There is a **big female population in Greek life**. There are not as many guys."

Q "Greek life at SU is very popular. **The Greek scene is a good option for many students who are looking to meet people** who share their same interests, but it is not essential in order to have a good time at SU."

Q "Almost all of my friends went Greek freshman year, but then they realized it was **cliquey, rich, and very snobby**."

Q "**Greek life is serious in Syracuse**. There are so many fraternities and sororities, it's disgusting. Greek life is almost like politics, and there are so many deep-seeded problems."

Q "Syracuse is **split down the middle between Greek life and independent life**. Most people find themselves pledging when they don't even think they're going to rush. Some people really talk it down, but in actuality, you can meet thousands of people by taking part in it."

The College Prowler Take On...
Academics

Greek life plays a very big role on campus. Whether you make friends with a person in a fraternity or sorority early on and proceed to spend a great deal of time at that house, or simply attend the frat parties on the weekends, students get used to Greek life from an outsider point of view very early on. Those students who choose to rush can only do so during their second semester of freshmen year. At SU, rushing is regulated so that you must go through the process of visiting every house before you make any decisions.

The Greek life for guys and girls differs greatly. First, it starts way back during the rush process. Guys generally are more laid-back about the whole routine. Although the process is the same, girls must go through a vigorous interview procedure and subsequent drama and politics as they choose which houses interest them, and the houses choose which freshmen interest them. After many tears and shouts of elation, the sororities have their pledge class. For guys, a simple "we want you here" is enough to get into the pledge class. But then the real drama begins. Although hazing is not allowed, many more legal, however still unpleasant, means of getting you to join their brotherhood and sisterhood are employed. After approximately eight weeks, you are a full brother or sister if you made it through the pledging, and the fun can really begin. Many Greek houses also participate in philanthropic and charity work that can both be fulfilling and good for your resume.

The College Prowler® Grade on

Greek Life: A

A high grade in Greek Life indicates that sororities and fraternities are not only present, but also active on campus. Other determining factors include the variety of houses available and the respect the Greek community receives from the rest of the campus.

Drug Scene

The Lowdown On...
Drug Scene

Most Prevalent Drugs on Campus:
Alcohol
Marijuana

Liquor-Related Referrals:
513

Liquor-Related Arrests:
41

Drug-Related Referrals:
168

Drug-Related Arrests:
53

Drug Counseling Programs:
Health enhancement program
Options program
Project CARE
Substance abuse prevention

Students Speak Out On...
Drug Scene

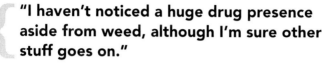

{ **"I haven't noticed a huge drug presence aside from weed, although I'm sure other stuff goes on."**

Q "**The drug scene is serious**. The biggest drugs on campus are marijuana, alcohol, and cocaine. The scope of the drug scene is one that seems to be far-reaching and widespread. The only way to seriously avoid it is to assimilate yourself into a group of friends who are drug-free. Otherwise, you will always find a druggie amongst the group."

Q "**The usual drugs are popular and available** (alcohol, weed). Cocaine is very popular in some Greek houses."

Q "Getting drugs on campus is as **easy as ordering a pizza**."

Q "Drugs are there. **You'll probably know at least one or two potheads** and maybe three or four other people who occasionally smoke pot. Harder drugs are pretty rare."

Q "The administration used to be pretty lax about drug use, but recently they've been starting to crack down. **You can still get away with a lot**, though."

Q "**There are a lot of drugs here**, but that's just like any college campus. I would say that the most common drug is weed, but there are several other drugs around, as well."

Q "Drugs aren't that big here. I was never into them, and neither were my friends. **It's really just a small group of people who use them**."

Q "**Some of the more wealthy students do cocaine**. Most people just smoke pot, though."

Q "Drugs exist, but **they're not overwhelming**."

Q "Drugs are definitely present. Of course, there's weed on campus, but there's also **ecstasy, coke, acid, and 'shrooms**. All that stuff is present anywhere you go, though, and you really don't notice it unless you are involved with it. The drug scene is no bigger than it is on any other college campus that I've visited."

The College Prowler Take On...
Drug Scene

The drug scene at Syracuse University is more than likely no different than at most schools across the United States. If a random poll of students were taken, a few would be serious drug users, some would be occasional users, and many would not use drugs at all. Marijuana is clearly the drug of choice for students, excluding alcohol, and it can be easily found on campus. Even if an individual is not an avid user, more than likely, he or she knows someone who sells weed.

At almost every party a student will attend, some party-goers will be smoking pot. It will be tough for a student to avoid being around marijuana for all four years at SU, but if the person truly doesn't want to use, it will be easy to find ways to evade it. The Options program in the Health Center is excellent for students who feel they have a problem and would like a private counselor to help them. The staff is knowledgeable and caring.

B-

The College Prowler® Grade on

Drug Scene: B-

A high grade in the Drug Scene indicates that drugs are not a noticeable part of campus life; drug use is not visible, and no pressure to use them seems to exist.

Campus
Strictness

The Lowdown On...
Campus Strictness

What Are You Most Likely to Get Caught Doing on Campus?
- Drinking in dorms
- Smoking in dorms
- Making too much noise in dorms
- Using a fake ID
- Drinking underage

Students Speak Out On...
Campus Strictness

"The RAs in the freshman dorms try to crack down on underage drinking, and if a party off campus get out of control, then the police will probably break it up. I guess you could say it's pretty strict."

Q "**Off-campus parties rarely get broken up** unless they are totally crazy. In the dorms, it usually depends on the RA assigned to your floor. But you can get kicked out of campus housing if you get caught with stuff a certain number of times. I would not say that it is extremely strict."

Q "In keeping with national standards, **SU enforces some strict policies regarding drugs and alcohol**. Three times caught with any amount of beer results in suspension for a year, and two times with any amount of weed yields the same punishment. Again, if you play it smart and make sure to cover your back, you should have no problem getting as messed up as you want without getting caught."

Q "I'm actually an RA, and we do a lot of the enforcing. Personally, I am not too strict. Some RAs are, but in general, **the attitude among the RAs that I know is to discourage abusive drinking**."

Q "**Dorms have a three-strikes-you're-out rule**. Bars are often raided for underage drinking, as well."

Q "**Judicial Affairs is serious**. Within your four years in Syracuse, you have three non-negotiable strikes. Be careful when carousing."

Q "Getting caught drinking when you're underage carries with it the penalty of having to write an essay or something along those lines. But **if you get busted for drugs, the penalty is more serious**."

Q "**Punishment can be fairly strict** if you are caught. Campus police break up parties routinely, but nobody really gets majorly busted."

Q "**The police are very strict here**, but I'm sure everyone does stuff on the down-low. It's rough if you get caught, but I don't know anybody who has ever been caught."

Q "**SU's policies are all enforced**; however, drug policies are much more severe than those for alcohol."

The College Prowler Take On...
Campus Strictness

Syracuse University has been cracking down on violations of the alcohol and drug policies on campus for a few years now. What used to be a fairly widely-regarded school for partying is now trying to change the image and focus efforts on reversing this trend. Although partying in frats and house parties are a generally safe proposition, drinking and smoking marijuana has grown increasingly risky. Students who may be making a lot of noise or inviting many different friends into the dorm can easily draw attention to themselves and subsequently be subject to a room check by resident advisors on duty at the time. If there is a continued problem with the room, Public Safety officers may be called and a date with Judicial Affairs could be imminent.

Getting written up by Public Safety is not considered getting written up by an RA, but both end up in the Judicial Affairs office. For your first alcohol violation, you'll be given a warning, then a letter will be written to your home for the second, and you'll get a one-semester suspension for the third. For drug violations, you'll first be placed on probation, then a one-semester suspension for the second. Other offenses carry different mandatory sentencing, although these rules are sometimes subject to change, and it is possible to plead your case before a group of peers. It is, however, safe to say you should avoid ever dealing with Judicial Affairs if at all possible.

The College Prowler® Grade on

Campus Strictness: C+

A high Campus Strictness grade implies an overall lenient atmosphere; police and RAs are fairly tolerant, and the administration's rules are flexible.

Parking

The Lowdown On...
Parking

Approximate Parking Permit Cost:
$400/year

SU Parking Services:
(315) 443-4652
http://bfasweb.syr.edu/parking
parkmail@syr.edu

Student Parking Lot?
Yes

Freshmen Allowed to Park?
Yes, with special permission

Parking Permits:
On-campus permit
Dorm permit with garage
Dorm permit without garage

Did You Know?

Best Places to Find a Parking Spot

During the morning, the Bird Library parking lot. In the afternoon, the only safe place to park and not get a ticket would be in the dorm parking lots. At night, you can park in one of the Marshall Street lots.

Good Luck Getting a Parking Spot Here!

Anywhere on campus. Technically, unless you have an on-campus parking pass (which you can't get as a freshman), you are not even allowed to drive your car on campus unless it is late at night.

Students Speak Out On...
Parking

"Parking is hard to find by the bars, but they did that deliberately to discourage drinking and driving."

Q "Parking sucks. **Freshmen can get permits for it**, but you really don't need a car during your freshman year."

Q "**Parking is a nightmare for freshmen**. They can't have a car unless they're in some sort of dire circumstances for which a car is required. You can get into a lot during your sophomore year for something like $400. I had my car up there from that point onwards."

Q "It's easy to park on campus, but **its tough to park and avoid a ticket**, though."

Q "Parking is bad at all schools, and Syracuse is no exception. **You can apply for a spot at a garage** in the area."

Q "**Parking is a big problem** for students on campus because there is no place to park between 8 a.m. and 9 p.m. You cannot drive on campus at all during those times, basically. The dorms are a short walk from the main campus, but if you do have a car and want to bring it with you, be prepared to pay as little as $50 for a lot a mile away from campus or $500 for a spot in a garage on campus."

Q "**It's not really easy to park on campus**. It's pretty crowded most of the time."

Q "You cannot park on campus unless you have an official permit to park in a particular parking lot. **When driving off campus, parking can be tight at times**, but is not a serious problem."

The College Prowler Take On...
Parking

The majority of freshmen will begin their college careers without cars. There is a reason for this. Walking to events like frat parties or off-campus parties, or heading down to Marshall Street for a bite to eat, must now become somewhat of a communal thing that involves more than just you and your best friend. You meet new people, enjoy some long conversations on the way to certain places, and can bond with the friends you have just met a few months before. And you will never need to drive to class, as all dorms are within a 10-minute walk from classes, even if you had a car.

Still, when it gets freezing, snowy, and windy sometime around November, it's nice to have a way to get around a little if you need to make a long trip. Parking is tough for those with a car, especially away from the dorms. Most dorms have a garage near them that students can park in for about $400 each year. It is near impossible to park on campus where your classes might be, and it is almost as hard to park on Marshall Street, especially at night. Students who choose to live on South Campus in their sophomore years will have a tougher time getting around, and relying on the bus at all times can be a pain. These students, as well as students who live off campus in their junior or senior years, should look into getting a car.

The College Prowler® Grade on

Parking: C-

A high grade in this section indicates that parking is both available and affordable, and that parking enforcement isn't overly severe.

Transportation

The Lowdown On...
Transportation

Ways to Get Around Town:

On Campus

There is a shuttle service that runs routes around campus. Unfortunately, these buses make very infrequent trips around SU.

SU Shuttle U Home
(315) 443-2224

Public Transportation

The CENTRO buses are free, and run to Carousel Mall, downtown Syracuse, and the train station, as well as across the entire campus.

CENTRO campus service
(315) 442-3400

Taxi Cabs

Cabs are are readily available and generally inexpensive. During winter break, the cab fare to the airport is set at $10 due to the influx of students going home.

(Taxi Cabs, continued)

Century Transportation
(315) 471-5151

AAA SU Taxi
(315) 478-8294

Car Rentals

Avis
national: (800) 831-2847
www.avis.com

Budget
national: (800) 527-0700
www.budget.com

Enterprise
national: (800) 736-8222
www.enterprise.com

Hertz
national: (800) 654-3131
www.hertz.com

National
national: (800) 227-7368
www.nationalcar.com

Best Ways to Get Around Town

Walk (in warmer weather)

Take a taxi

Ways to Get Out of Town:

Airport

Hancock International Airport

1000 Colonel Eileen Collins Boulevard

Syracuse, NY 13212

(315) 454-3263

www.syrairport.org/index.cfm

Airlines Serving Syracuse

American Eagle
(800) 433-7300
www.americanairlines.com

Continental Express
(800) 525-0280
www.continental.com

Delta
(800) 221-1212
www.delta-air.com

JetBlue Airways
(800) 538- 2583
www.jetblue.com

Northwest
(800) 225-2525
www.nwa.com

Transmeridian Airlines
(866) 435-9862
www.transmeridian-airlines. com

United Express
(800) 241-6522
www.united.com

(Airlines, continued)

US Airways
(800) 428-4322
www.usairways.com

How to Get to the Airport

Take I-81 North to Exit 27

Continue on Airport Boulevard/Colonel Eileen Collins Boulevard

Follow signs to parking and terminal.

Greyhound

131 P and C Pkwy
Syracuse, NY 13208
(315) 472-5339
(800) 231-2222
www.greyhound.com

Amtrak

131 P & C Pkwy
Syracuse, NY 13208
(315) 477-1152
www.amtrak.com

Travel Agents

Absolute Travel
1112 First North Street
(315) 477-1389

Liberty Travel
3550 West Genesee Street #2
(315) 488-3191

University Travel Inc.
129 Marshall Street
(315) 474-4871

> **"As an SU student, you won't really have any need to go off campus much, but there is a decent city-wide bus system called the CENTRO."**

Q "If you know the bus schedule and the place you want to go, it's not bad. Otherwise, **bring a book, because trips can take a while**, especially if you hop the wrong bus to Carousel Mall."

Q "**Public transportation is very efficient**. They run their business very professionally and efficiently. Anywhere on campus, it's always easy to find the nearest bus stop because you are always within five minutes of a stop."

Q "**You can take a bus to anywhere on campus**. You won't have any problems with that."

Q "There is public transportation that runs from SU to the big mall located nearby once every hour on the weekends. Other than that, **you'll find that taxis are the easiest way to get around unless you have a car**. The buses are good to get back and forth from North Campus to South Campus, but I haven't used them for anything else."

Q "**Cabs are readily available**. The bus system is okay, but really slow."

Q "**You can always call a cab or take a city bus**, and if you don't have a car, someone you know probably will."

Q "**Taxis are convenient but expensive**. I have never taken the bus anywhere, and I don't know anyone who has."

The College Prowler Take On...
Transportation

Getting around campus is fairly easy if you pay attention to the many schedules and signs provided for students. Syracuse University has a convenient bus service that shuttles students to and from South Campus, as well as around main campus. There are also three bus stops on campus for trips to such places as downtown Syracuse and the Carousel Mall. As long as you know the schedule, you will certainly do fine getting around campus.

Also, taxis are always readily available. Some students hail a cab to go to the airport, which can be fairly inexpensive. Other students like to use cabs as their designated driver when they go to bars and frats on campus, and they are always available late at night. Buses, trains, and planes are also convenient, as long as you can make your way to either Hancock Airport or the Transportation Center. Both are within a 10-minute drive from the SU campus. Although the airport is small, there are flights that leave from Hancock to almost every destination an SU student would need to go.

The College Prowler® Grade on

Transportation: A-

A high grade for Transportation indicates that campus buses, public buses, cabs, and rental cars are readily-available and affordable. Other determining factors include proximity to an airport and the necessity of transportation.

Weather

The Lowdown On...
Weather

Average Temperature:
Fall: 50.7 °F
Winter: 22.4 °F
Spring: 45.7 °F
Summer: 69.4 °F

Average Precipitation:
Fall: 3.2 in.
Winter: 2.3 in.
Spring: 3.3 in.
Summer: 3.8 in.

Students Speak Out On...
Weather

"All I can say is get ready for a type of cold you have never before experienced. There is sporadic snowing in May! Bring every piece of warm clothing you have or you will never make it out alive."

Q "**SU is notorious for its severe winter weather**. From November until April, it snows, sleets, and rains approximately three times a week. The temperature and precipitation are not the biggest weather problems at SU in my opinion, but rather the wind that goes along with these conditions."

Q "**The weather is very unpredictable**. One day, it'll snow, and the next day, it'll be sunny and 85 degrees. So prepare for everything when you're packing."

Q "It snows a lot; **you'll inevitably get tired of the snow** and all the cold weather. Be prepared to have a rough winter."

Q "**The weather here sucks**. It snows from October until about April or May. It's always cold and gray, and rarely sunny or warm. When it does get sunny or warm, people freak out. The weather is the thing that I hate the most about going to school in Syracuse."

Q "**There are some beautiful days at the beginning of the year** and then again towards the end, but it tends to go from one extreme to the other. When it is cold out, it is extremely cold, and when it is hot, it is way too hot."

Q "I won't lie: **winter weather in Syracuse sucks**. But you'll find that from August until October, and sometimes even into November, the weather is great. It's still sunny out and even into late October, the temperature can be as high as the 60s."

Q "**The weather is cold**! The polar ice cap of central New York would have to be Syracuse. Expect snow, wind, ice, rain, and no sun!"

Q "**Bring warm clothes**. When you first get here it will be warm until early November. Then, it is freezing forever."

Q "The weather is terrible. **It's the worst part about attending SU**. I'm not going to lie. My freshman year was horrible. It's snowy and icy and just plain bad. But then again, I don't like snow much."

Q "**Cold. Lots of cold**. But it makes you appreciate the warmer months a lot more than if it were always warm."

The College Prowler Take On...
Weather

Syracuse is known for its snow, but students will find it far easier to adjust to a few inches constantly on the ground than to the wind and cold they will encounter. It will get very cold. By November, it will be in the 40s regularly; by December, it will be below freezing. With the wind chill factor, especially in January and February, temperatures can drop way below zero. It isn't a fun time walking to class across the quad with a temperature of negative 10 degrees and wind gusts reaching more than 30 miles per hour. Also, it makes the occasional 50 degree day in March seem like a tropical vacation.

There is no nice way to say it—if you like beautiful weather, head to Miami or California. At Syracuse, no one came because he or she likes making snow angels or being whipped in the face with wind. Even snow bunnies will be disappointed in the lack of skiing the Syracuse area has to offer. If SU is your choice for college, it most certainly should be for some other reason than the weather. As far as clothes, make sure you do have mostly warm clothes, and dress in layers. Do, however, bring a couple outfits of shorts and short sleeves, as you should be prepared to jump at any opportunity to abandon your hoodie, warm hat, earmuffs, and mittens.

D+

The College Prowler® Grade on
Weather: D+

A high Weather grade designates that temperatures are mild and rarely reach extremes, that the campus tends to be sunny rather than rainy, and that weather is fairly consistent rather than unpredictable.

Report Card Summary

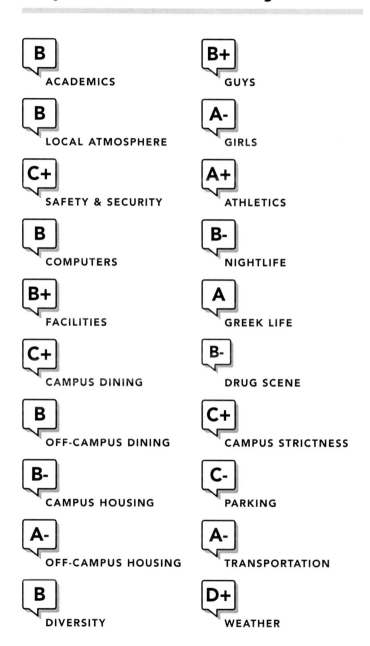

B ACADEMICS

B LOCAL ATMOSPHERE

C+ SAFETY & SECURITY

B COMPUTERS

B+ FACILITIES

C+ CAMPUS DINING

B OFF-CAMPUS DINING

B- CAMPUS HOUSING

A- OFF-CAMPUS HOUSING

B DIVERSITY

B+ GUYS

A- GIRLS

A+ ATHLETICS

B- NIGHTLIFE

A GREEK LIFE

B- DRUG SCENE

C+ CAMPUS STRICTNESS

C- PARKING

A- TRANSPORTATION

D+ WEATHER

Overall Experience

Students Speak Out On...
Overall Experience

"I'm at the Newhouse School of Communications, so I'm glad with my choice. I know it's a great school to get into. I want to be a director or producer some day."

"Let's just say that I've had friends from home come to visit and they've decided **it's blown away their colleges**. I've even had one of them transfer to Syracuse last year because he had such a good time visiting."

"SU is a great school. It's in a city, but not a huge city. Syrcause can be ghetto, but **SU is like its own community**. If you wanted to, you could never leave the campus."

Q "For my major, Syracuse has one of the best schools in the nation. If it wasn't for that, I wouldn't come here to be **tortured by the winters** that last from October to May or the roving bands of sorority girls."

Q "Syracuse is the greatest place in the world. **There is no other place I'd rather be right now**, and I'm hesitant to even think about leaving college. I absolutely love every single thing about this place, even the weather!"

Q "I love SU. **Be sure to pick your major early** because if you switch from, let's say, the College of Arts and Sciences into the VPA program, you could get caught having to stay an extra year due to different program setups. I love it there, and I wish I were back there now."

Q "I can't say enough good things about this place. I've loved every second of it. **Syracuse is just so much fun**, and you're getting a great education at the same time."

Q "I loved Syracuse and **wish I had stayed there**. I went to Penn State for two years, and it just didn't compare."

Q "SU is a really good school academically. **I love the program that I'm in, but that's about it**. I hate the people here, I hate the atmosphere, and I hate the weather, but if you are into Greek life and snobs, I would say that SU is the school for you."

Q "I love it here. **I don't want college to end**."

The College Prowler Take On...
Overall Experience

SU has a laundry list of good qualities about it and very few flaws. The main thing to remember is that SU and its students refuse to be pigeonholed. There are so many varying interests at Syracuse University, as well as a broad array of extracurricular activities. People can't even agree on what major is the most prestigious (although many claim communications or architecture). Still, although there is a broad range of people at SU, there usually is a consensus on one thing: people at Syracuse University really like it. Sure, there are different reasons, but almost everyone who spends a few years at SU enjoys it.

Some like the choices in classes, while others like the prominent sports teams on campus. Some like the appeal of a real college campus in the middle of a big city. No one comes for the weather. And besides the few reasons a student will specifically seek out Syracuse University, there are a broad number of factors that keep students here. The on-campus and off-campus housing is excellent, the computer facilities are top-notch, and the nightlife can be a major draw. Also, students generally have a lot of genuinely interesting events going on around campus. Whatever the reason, students who come to SU tend to stay here.

The Inside Scoop

The Lowdown On...
The Inside Scoop

Syracuse Slang:

Know the slang, know the school. The following is a list of things you really need to know before coming to Syracuse. The more of these words you know, the better off you'll be.

Campus D – Campus Delivery, the University-run delivery service. They charge your meal to your Supercard and deliver to dorms.

The DO – The *Daily Orange* is the student-run campus newspaper. It is the most widely read college newspaper in the country.

The Dome – The Dome is what SU students call the Carrier Dome, the place where SU's men's basketball, men's lacrosse, and football teams play home games.

The Dot – This is the nickname for food.com, the dining area located in the Newhouse School.

Frat Row – This is the name for the portion of Comstock Avenue between Euclid Avenue and Dellplain Hall. Many parties, especially ones attended by freshmen, are in this area.

→

The Ghetto – This generally refers to the communities directly surrounding the SU campus. More specifically, the area around the Brewster/Boland dorms and beyond Comstock Avenue.

K-Rads – This is the nickname for Konrad's, one of the better-known bars near the SU campus. Before it closed, it was a favorite hang out for many SU students.

M-Street – M-Street is a shortened term coined for Marshall Street. M-Street is the place where many bars and restaurants that are directly next to campus can be found.

The Mount – This term is a shortened version of Mount Olympus Drive. The Mount is the street where two dorms, Day and Flint Halls, are located. It is situated on the top of a big hill, and it is generally known for housing some of SU's richer freshmen.

OCC – These are the initials of Onondaga Community College, which is the community college located in Syracuse.

The Quad – This is the area in the middle of the SU campus. It is a grassy, park-like place (when it isn't covered with snow) where students go to relax, play Frisbee, and hang out.

Red Shirts – This is a friendly nickname for people who work for Residential Security (RSAs). These individuals sit at the entrance to all dorms on campus checking ID cards from 8 p.m. to 8 a.m. every day. They can be identified by their red shirts, hence the name.

South – A shortened term for South Campus, this is the area of Syracuse that is south of the main campus, and it houses many students in apartment-like dorms.

The Toilet Bowl – This is a nickname for Haven Hall. It acquired this name because of its striking resemblance to the bathroom fixture.

Townie – This term refers to a local resident of Syracuse. It can often be seen and used as a negative term.

Things I Wish I Knew Before Coming to Syracuse

- How to manage time better.
- Exactly just how cold it can get here.
- The fact that bars are frequently being raided, making it unsafe to go there underage or with a fake ID.
- Homework, although not often a lengthy process, is important to your final grade in many courses.

Tips to Succeed at Syracuse

- You should really take a few hours of each day to study. It won't affect your free time in the least bit, especially if you get the bulk of the studying done before 9 or 10 p.m.
- Visit your professors during the semester. Make sure they know you. It will help. They make themselves available to you, and you have to take advantage of that.
- Spend time in between classes to get work done so you have less to do at night or over the weekend. If you're a morning person, you might want to get some work done in the mornings before class starts.
- Go to class. Go to all of your classes as much as you can. It's okay to miss some days, but once you make a habit out of it, it's hard to break.
- Meet as many people as you can the first month. No one knows anyone in the beginning of the year. It can be the most important time to gain the friends you will have for your freshman year, and maybe even the friends you will have for your entire college career.
- Join a few clubs and organizations that interest you, but not every club and organization that interests you. If you find something that you enjoy, and there truly is something for everyone here, you should most certainly pursue it.
- Watch out for getting a cold in December when the real cold weather starts. Take Vitamin C supplements.
- If you don't like your roommate, don't hang out with him or her. It won't affect your life too much if you don't let it.

Syracuse Urban Legends

Kissing Bench – There is an old stone bench next to the Hall of Languages built in 1912. Legend has it that if a couple kisses on the bench, they will eventually marry.

Saltine Warrior – In 1931, the *Orange Peel*, the SU newspaper at the time, published a story about the unearthing of the skeleton of a famous Indian Chief and his valuable artifacts on the SU campus. The story was later deemed a hoax, but the Saltine Warrior, as he was known, remained the Syracuse University mascot until 1978. Now there is a statue of the Saltine Warrior in front of Carnegie Library.

Underground Passageways – Students, since freshman year, have mused over the fact that there may be underground tunnels connecting many buildings on the SU campus. This would be great, not to mention extremely convenient, considering the weather in Syracuse. However, the only confirmed connecting tunnels are between Day and Flint Halls, Lawrinson and Sadler Halls, and Brewster and Boland Halls. No tunnels have been found to interconnect between all of the halls.

Traditions

44

The number 44 has been worn by nine football players, three of which have earned All-American honors (Jim Brown, Ernie Davis, and Floyd Little). The number was also worn by both Derrick Coleman and John Wallace, two of the greatest basketball stars in SU history. For this reason, the number 44 has come to encompass all that is successful with both SU sports and Syracuse University in general. As you might have noticed, all numbers having to do with SU were changed to begin with 44, and the zip code was changed to 13244. It is somewhat of a lucky, if not legendary, number for students and faculty alike at SU.

Block Party

This is a weekend event in April that brings a top musical talent to SU, as well as sometimes having carnival-type rides. The Block Party has been diminishing in recent years.

Crouse Chimes

The chimes on top of Crouse College building were installed in 1889 and renovated in 1981. Now, the chimes can be heard twice a day, and sometimes more on special occasions.

The Color Orange

The color orange was adopted by Syracuse University in 1890, making it the only college in the country at the time with one official color. Although orange might not be the color of choice for some of the SU students today, it certainly beats the color scheme it replaced: pea green and rose pink.

Otto the Orange

The issue of this school mascot is one deeply-rooted in history. The first mascot of SU was the Saltine Warrior, which remained as such until 1978 when Native Americans complained it was disrespectful to their culture. After the Saltine Warrior was abandoned, SU began a lengthy search for a new mascot. Their first selection was a Roman warrior-type character that year who was dismissed after the first football game that SU lost. After that, SU proposed ideas ranging from a troll to a "Beast from the East" monster and even an abominable snowman. Eventually, they decided on the Orangemen, but in 1995 the administration proposed changing it to a wolf. This decision was met with disdain from the student body, so in 1997 it was made official that the team was the Orange, and Otto the Orange would remain the University's mascot.

Finding a Job or Internship

The Lowdown On...
Finding a Job or Internship

Internships and jobs are often found by using the resources within your individual school at Syracuse. Career Services is located in Schine Student Center and can provide you with general information. Keep your eye out for internship and job fairs that SU holds about twice a year. Also, there are many jobs and internships in the Syracuse area that can help you once your college life is over.

Advice

Look to get an internship in your junior and or senior years, at least. These look great for your resume, as well as provide valuable hands-on training for your field. Don't wait until the spring to start searching for an internship, either. You should have applications in to possible employers by January. Be aggressive and make your own contacts, and you will suceed.

Career Center Resources & Services

Syracuse University Internship Program
113 Euclid Avenue
(315) 443-4271
http://internships.syr.edu

Center for Career Services
Schine Student Center, Room 235
303 University Place
(315) 443-3616
clreutli@syr.edu

Average Salary Information

Approximately $30,000/year, factoring in all majors
and schools.

Grads Who Enter the Job Market Within

6 Months: 92%

1 Year: N/A

Firms That Most Frequently Hire Grads

Accenture, Bloomingdale's, CIGNA, Citigroup, Deloitte &
Touche, Ernst & Young, ESPN, General Electric, IBM, KPMG,
Liberty Mutual, Lockheed Martin, Macy's, Merrill Lynch, Ogilvy
& Mather, PricewaterhouseCoopers, Raytheon, St. Joseph's
Hospital, Strong Memorial Hospital, Syracuse City School
District (and other school districts), Teach For America, Time
Warner Cable, UTC Carrier

Did You Know?

The Career Center also offers the **Career Services
Network**, which has many student resources,
including a career-management model, a six-stage
career-development model, e-recruiting, testing
choices, and enhancement of job search skills.

Alumni

The Lowdown On...
Alumni

Web Site:
www.syr.edu/alumni

E-Mail:
sualumni@syr.edu

Office:
Office of Alumni Relations
Syracuse University
401 University Place
(315) 443-3258

Services Available:
Alumni Directory
Awards
Career Services
Publications

Major Alumni Events

Homecoming
Gatherings in major cities
Reunions
Tours

Alumni Publications

Orangebytes — a monthy e-newsletter containing SU-related
news and events

Did You Know?

Famous SU Alumni

Marv Albert – Sportscaster

Jim Brown – Former athlete; advocate

Dick Clark – TV Host and CEO of Dick Clark
Productions

Bob Costas – Sportscaster

Taye Diggs – Actor

Thom Filicia – Interior designer for *Queer Eye for the Straight
Guy*

Ted Koppel – Newscaster

William Safire – *New York Times* columnist

Aaron Sorkin – TV producer/director; creator of the
West Wing

Jerry Stiller – Actor

Mike Tirico – Sportscaster

Vanessa Williams – Singer/actress; first black Miss America

Student Organizations

This represents a sample of each type of student organization. For a full list, you can go to *http://students.syr.edu/glel/recognizedorganizations.html* or call (315) 443-2718.

Ad Club

African American Male Congress – *http://students.syr.edu/aamc*

African Student Union – *http://aas.syr.edu/students.html*

Anthropology Club Architecture Student Organizations – *http://soa.syr.edu/students/organizations.html*

Asian Event Group

Black and Latino Information Studies Support – *http://blists.syr.edu*

Black Box Players

Black Communications Society

The Black Voice – *http://students.syr.edu/bvoice*

Campus Crusade for Christ – *http://web.syr.edu/~odmay/cccw.htm*

Chabad House Jewish Student Organization – *http://web.syr.edu/~chabad*

College Democrats

College of Nursing Council

College Republicans

Commuters' Organization

Composition and Culture Rhetoric

Graduate Student Organization

Danceworks

The *Daily Orange* – *www.dailyorange.com*

Diversity in the Arts English Graduate Organization – *http://english.syr.edu/graduate/graduate.htm*

Equal Time Magazine

Equestrian Club

Fashion Association of Design Students

Fashion's Conscience – *http://students.syr.edu/fc*

Fellowship of Christian Athletes

Fencing Club

First Year Players

Global Nomads

Graduate Student Organization – *http://students.syr.edu/gso*

Habitat for Humanity – *http://web.syr.edu/~habhum/syrword.html*

Haitian American Students Association

Hill TV (SU student-run TV station) – *http://uutv.syr.edu*

Jewish Student Union Juggling Club – *http://students.syr.edu/juggling/clubmeetings.html*

Institute of Electrical & Electronics Engineers

Inter Fraternity Sorority Council

International Management Association

International Students Consortium

Intervarsity Christian Fellowship

Irish American Society

Islamic Society

Juggling Association

Kappa Kappa Psi

Korean Student Association

La Fuerza

Latin American Law Student Association

Latinos Unidos

Latter-day Saint Student Association

Linux Users Group

Literary Society

Local Students Union

Lutheran Campus Ministry

Marine Science Association

Mathematics Education Student Association – *http://soeweb. syr.edu/mathedmesa.htm*

Medieval Re-creation Society

Model United Nations

Mustard Seed

NAACP

National Council for International Health

National Society of Collegeiate Scholars

Navigators Christian Fellowship

Outing Club

Outreach Educators for Youth Primate Alliance

Pakistani Students Association

Phi Alpha Delta

Photography Club

Pre Dental Society

Pre Medical Society

Programming Council

R.O.C. Chinese Student Association

Real Life: Campus Crusade for Christ

Red Cross Volunteers

Running Club

Russian Cultural Club

SAR

SHA Student Government

Shelter Legal Services

Sikh Association

Singapore Collegiate Society

Ski Club

Skydiving Club

Slow Children at Play

SMG Student Government
Society for Middle Eastern Studies
Society of Hispanic Professional Engineers
Society of Women Engineers
South Campus RHA
Speak Easy
Spectrum
Spontaneous Combustion
SSW Student Organization
Stage Troupe
Student Social Science Group
Student Union
Taiwanese American Student Association
TARANG Indian Student's Association
Tau Beta Pi Association
Tau Beta Sigma
Team Learning Organization
Terpsichore
Treblemakers
Tru Sole
Undergraduate Economics Association
Undergraduates for a Better Education
Vietnamese Student Association
Warren Towers RHA
Women's Center
Women's Interfaith Action Group
Women's Law Association

The Best & Worst

The Ten **BEST** Things About SU

1	Midnights on Marshall Street
2	Kimmel Food Court at 2 a.m. on a Saturday night
3	SU's nine prestigious undergrad colleges
4	The national championship-winning basketball team
5	Happy hour
6	Hanging out in Panasci Lounge during a blizzard
7	After-hours frat parties that start when the bars close
8	The wide variety of extracurricular activities
9	Dorm perks (like snack bars, garages, game rooms, and coed-by-alternating-rooms housing)
10	Orange spirit in the Carrier Dome

The Ten WORST Things About SU

1 Windy afternoons on Marshall Street

2 Dining hall food

3 Teaching assistants who barely speak English, and part-time professors who don't like their jobs

4 The very average football team

5 Bar raids

6 Being able to walk into class and have the weather be 30 degrees and sunny, and then walking out of class an hour later to find a blizzard, sub-zero weather, and winds up to 30 miles per hour

7 Not clear enough? The weather is awful!

8 The outskirts of campus are not as safe as one would like

9 Dorm downfalls, like the endless stairs to the Mount, the "ghetto" areas of Brewster and Boland, and the "middle of nowhere" feel of Lawrinson and Sadler

10 Pick up that Freshmen 15 anyway

Visiting

The Lowdown On...
Visiting

Hotel Information:

Candlewood Suites Syracuse
5414 South Bay Road
(315) 454-8999
www.candlewoodsuites.com
Distance from Campus:
6 miles
Price Range: $55–$99

Comfort Inn Syracuse
6491 Thompson Road
(315) 437-0222
Distance from Campus:
6 miles
Price Range: $62–$99

→

Days Inn Syracuse University

6609 Thompson Road

(315) 437-5998

www.daysinn.com

Distance from Campus:
6 miles

Price Range: $39–$58

Quality Inn North Syracuse

1308 Buckley Road

(315) 451-1212

Distance from Campus:
7 miles

Price Range: $80–$150

Red Roof Syracuse

6614 North Thompson Road

(315) 437-3309

www.redroof.com

Distance from Campus:
6 miles

Price Range: $40–$60

Sheraton Syracuse University

801 University Avenue

(315) 475-3000

www.syracusesheraton.com

Distance from Campus:
On campus

Price Range: $109–$329

Take a Campus Virtual Tour

http://emc.syr.edu/tour

To Schedule a Group Information Session or Interview

(315) 443-3611

Campus Tours

Tours and information sessions for prospective students are offered every Saturday. Information sessions begin at 10 a.m., and tours begin at 11 a.m. Also, in January–March, there are daily tours that begin at 12 p.m. and 3 p.m, and for admitted students, there are tours in March and April. You must call in advance to reserve your spot for all these tours and sessions.

Overnight Visits

There is no official program in place for overnight visits, but if you are an admitted student, you can arrange for an overnight stay by contacting your respective department/school.

Directions to Campus

Driving from the North

- Take Interstate-81 South to Syracuse, Harrison/Adams Street exit (exit 18).
- Bear left, follow signs for Syracuse University, at the bottom of the exit ramp.

Driving from the South

- Take Interstate-81 North to Syracuse, Harrison/Adams Street exit (exit 18).
- At bottom of ramp, make a right onto East Adams Street and follow signs for Syracuse University.

Driving from the East

- Take Interstate-90 West to Exit 34A.
- Take Syracuse ramp to Interstate-481 South.
- Take Interstate-481 South to Intestate-690 West.
- Take Interstate-690 West to the Teall Avenue exit. Bear left at bottom of exit ramp.
- Follow Teall Avenue to Erie Boulevard. Make right onto Erie Boulevard.
- Turn left onto University Avenue, and follow signs for Syracuse University.

Driving from the West

- Take Interstate-90 East to or Interstate-690 East to Interstate-81 South to Syracuse.
- Exit at Harrison/Adams Street (exit 18).
- Bear left, follow signs for Syracuse University at the bottom of the exit ramp.

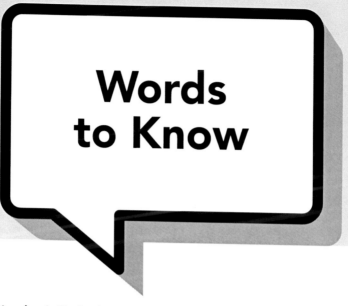

Words to Know

Academic Probation – A suspension imposed on a student if he or she fails to keep up with the school's minimum academic requirements. Those unable to improve their grades after receiving this warning can face dismissal.

Beer Pong/Beirut – A drinking game involving cups of beer arranged in a pyramid shape on each side of a table. The goal is to get a ping pong ball into one of the opponent's cups by throwing the ball or hitting it with a paddle. If the ball lands in a cup, the opponent is required to drink the beer.

Bid – An invitation from a fraternity or sorority to 'pledge' (join) that specific house.

Blue-Light Phone – Brightly-colored phone posts with a blue light bulb on top. These phones exist for security purposes and are located at various outside locations around most campuses. In an emergency, a student can pick up one of these phones (free of charge) to connect with campus police or a security escort.

Campus Police – Police who are specifically assigned to a given institution. Campus police are typically not regular city officers; they are employed by the university in a full-time capacity.

Club Sports – A level of sports that falls somewhere between varsity and intramural. If a student is unable to commit to a varsity team but has a lot of passion for athletics, a club sport could be a better, less intense option. Even less demanding, intramural (IM) sports often involve no traveling and considerably less time.

Cocaine – An illegal drug. Also known as "coke" or "blow," cocaine often resembles a white crystalline or powdery substance. It is highly addictive and dangerous.

Common Application – An application with which students can apply to multiple schools.

Course Registration – The period of official class selection for the upcoming quarter or semester. Prior to registration, it is best to prepare several back-up courses in case a particular class becomes full. If a course is full, students can place themselves on the waitlist, although this still does not guarantee entry.

Division Athletics – Athletic classifications range from Division I to Division III. Division IA is the most competitive, while Division III is considered to be the least competitive.

Dorm – A dorm (or dormitory) is an on-campus housing facility. Dorms can provide a range of options from suite-style rooms to more communal options that include shared bathrooms. Most first-year students live in dorms. Some upperclassmen who wish to stay on campus also choose this option.

Early Action – An application option with which a student can apply to a school and receive an early acceptance response without a binding commitment. This system is becoming less and less available.

Early Decision – An application option that students should use only if they are certain they plan to attend the school in question. If a student applies using the early decision option and is admitted, he or she is required and bound to attend that university. Admission rates are usually higher among students who apply through early decision, as the student is clearly indicating that the school is his or her first choice.

Ecstasy – An illegal drug. Also known as "E" or "X," ecstasy looks like a pill and most resembles an aspirin. Considered a party drug, ecstasy is very dangerous and can be deadly.

Ethernet – An extremely fast Internet connection available in most university-owned residence halls. To use an Ethernet connection properly, a student will need a network card and cable for his or her computer.

Fake ID – A counterfeit identification card that contains false information. Most commonly, students get fake IDs with altered birthdates so that they appear to be older than 21 (and therefore of legal drinking age). Even though it is illegal, many college students have fake IDs in hopes of purchasing alcohol or getting into bars.

Frosh – Slang for "freshman" or "freshmen."

Hazing – Initiation rituals administered by some fraternities or sororities as part of the pledging process. Many universities have outlawed hazing due to its degrading, and sometimes dangerous, nature.

Intramurals (IMs) – A popular, and usually free, sport league in which students create teams and compete against one another. These sports vary in competitiveness and can include a range of activities—everything from billiards to water polo. IM sports are a great way to meet people with similar interests.

Keg – Officially called a half-barrel, a keg contains roughly 200 12-ounce servings of beer.

LSD – An illegal drug, also known as acid, this hallucinogenic drug most commonly resembles a tab of paper.

Marijuana – An illegal drug, also known as weed or pot; along with alcohol, marijuana is one of the most commonly-found drugs on campuses across the country.

Major –The focal point of a student's college studies; a specific topic that is studied for a degree. Examples of majors include physics, English, history, computer science, economics, business, and music. Many students decide on a specific major before arriving on campus, while others are simply "undecided" until declaring a major. Those who are extremely interested in two areas can also choose to double major.

Meal Block – The equivalent of one meal. Students on a meal plan usually receive a fixed number of meals per week. Each meal, or "block," can be redeemed at the school's dining facilities in place of cash. Often, a student's weekly allotment of meal blocks will be forfeited if not used.

Minor – An additional focal point in a student's education. Often serving as a complement or addition to a student's main area of focus, a minor has fewer requirements and prerequisites to fulfill than a major. Minors are not required for graduation from most schools; however some students who want to explore many different interests choose to pursue both a major and a minor.

Mushrooms – An illegal drug. Also known as "'shrooms," this drug resembles regular mushrooms but is extremely hallucinogenic.

Off-Campus Housing – Housing from a particular landlord or rental group that is not affiliated with the university. Depending on the college, off-campus housing can range from extremely popular to non-existent. Students who choose to live off campus are typically given more freedom, but they also have to deal with possible subletting scenarios, furniture, bills, and other issues. In addition to these factors, rental prices and distance often affect a student's decision to move off campus.

Office Hours – Time that teachers set aside for students who have questions about coursework. Office hours are a good forum for students to go over any problems and to show interest in the subject material.

Pledging – The early phase of joining a fraternity or sorority, pledging takes place after a student has gone through rush and received a bid. Pledging usually lasts between one and two semesters. Once the pledging period is complete and a particular student has done everything that is required to become a member, that student is considered a brother or sister. If a fraternity or a sorority would decide to "haze" a group of students, this initiation would take place during the pledging period.

Private Institution – A school that does not use tax revenue to subsidize education costs. Private schools typically cost more than public schools and are usually smaller.

Prof – Slang for "professor."

Public Institution – A school that uses tax revenue to subsidize education costs. Public schools are often a good value for in-state residents and tend to be larger than most private colleges.

Quarter System (or Trimester System) – A type of academic calendar system. In this setup, students take classes for three academic periods. The first quarter usually starts in late September or early October and concludes right before Christmas. The second quarter usually starts around early to mid–January and finishes up around March or April. The last academic quarter, or "third quarter," usually starts in late March or early April and finishes up in late May or Mid-June. The fourth quarter is summer. The major difference between the quarter system and semester system is that students take more, less comprehensive courses under the quarter calendar.

RA (Resident Assistant) – A student leader who is assigned to a particular floor in a dormitory in order to help to the other students who live there. An RA's duties include ensuring student safety and providing assistance wherever possible.

Recitation – An extension of a specific course; a review session. Some classes, particularly large lectures, are supplemented with mandatory recitation sessions that provide a relatively personal class setting.

Rolling Admissions – A form of admissions. Most commonly found at public institutions, schools with this type of policy continue to accept students throughout the year until their class sizes are met. For example, some schools begin accepting students as early as December and will continue to do so until April or May.

Room and Board – This figure is typically the combined cost of a university-owned room and a meal plan.

Room Draw/Housing Lottery – A common way to pick on-campus room assignments for the following year. If a student decides to remain in university-owned housing, he or she is assigned a unique number that, along with seniority, is used to determine his or her housing for the next year.

Rush – The period in which students can meet the brothers and sisters of a particular chapter and find out if a given fraternity or sorority is right for them. Rushing a fraternity or a sorority is not a requirement at any school. The goal of rush is to give students who are serious about pledging a feel for what to expect.

Semester System – The most common type of academic calendar system at college campuses. This setup typically includes two semesters in a given school year. The fall semester starts around the end of August or early September and concludes before winter vacation. The spring semester usually starts in mid-January and ends in late April or May.

Student Center/Rec Center/Student Union – A common area on campus that often contains study areas, recreation facilities, and eateries. This building is often a good place to meet up with fellow students; depending on the school, the student center can have a huge role or a non-existent role in campus life.

Student ID – A university-issued photo ID that serves as a student's key to school-related functions. Some schools require students to show these cards in order to get into dorms, libraries, cafeterias, and other facilities. In addition to storing meal plan information, in some cases, a student ID can actually work as a debit card and allow students to purchase things from bookstores or local shops.

Suite – A type of dorm room. Unlike dorms that feature communal bathrooms shared by the entire floor, suites offer bathrooms shared only among the suite. Suite-style dorm rooms can house anywhere from two to ten students.

TA (Teacher's Assistant) – An undergraduate or grad student who helps in some manner with a specific course. In some cases, a TA will teach a class, assist a professor, grade assignments, or conduct office hours.

Undergraduate – A student in the process of studying for his or her bachelor's degree.

ABOUT THE AUTHOR

Understandably, this book is not one that keeps you up late at night in dire anticipation as to what is on the next page, or a book that you sit down to read a few pages of and find yourself overwhelmed by its power. Hopefully, though, this book provides you the information you sought after and will supply you with a valuable reference tool in your years at Syracuse University. I also hope you enjoyed reading this book as much as I enjoyed writing it. When I graduate from SU, I look forward to expanding my writing ability. As a broadcast journalism major who is also a columnist for the *Daily Orange*, I thoroughly relished in this opportunity to broaden my horizons and put my name on a book of my own. It was an experience I enjoyed, especially as I was able to write about Syracuse University, a place I have tremendous respect for and have a great time attending. This has also been a great learning experience for me as a writer. If you have any questions, including any specific points that were not included in this guide, please e-mail me at stevekrakauer@collegeprowler.com.

I would like to thank many people who have had a major effect on both me and this project. First, I want to thank my parents, whose support through this and everything else is always unwavering. Thank you for keeping your criticism constructive and your praise sincere. Hopefully, this will be the first of many times where you will see my gratitude to you on this public of a stage. I also want to thank my little sister, Alison, who I love very much. Thank you to everyone at the *Westfield Leader* for giving me the opportunity to have people read my writing. I learned so much during my three years with you all. Thank you to the *Daily Orange* for being an open outlet for my voice to be heard. Also, I want to thank Elizabeth Muller who taught me so much during two years of the toughest English class I have ever been a part of. You truly gave me the strength to believe that someday the words "by Steve Krakauer" would be attached to a book. Thank you to Jon Adler, George Azar, Missy Burlin, Matt Chazanow, Courtney Dolloff, Rob Daurio, Bridget Fitzpatrick, Ron Levy, and Ben Kahn for their help with this project. Finally, I want to thank everyone at College Prowler for giving me this opportunity.

Steve Krakauer

California Colleges

California dreamin'?
This book is a must have for you!

CALIFORNIA COLLEGES
7¼" X 10", 762 Pages Paperback
$29.95 Retail
1-59658-501-3

Stanford, UC Berkeley, Caltech—California is home
to some of America's greatest institutes of higher
learning. *California Colleges* gives the lowdown on 24
of the best, side by side, in one prodigious volume.

New England Colleges

Looking for peace in the Northeast?
Pick up this regional guide to New England!

NEW ENGLAND COLLEGES
7¼" X 10", 1015 Pages Paperback
$29.95 Retail
1-59658-504-8

New England is the birthplace of many prestigious universities, and with so many to choose from, picking the right school can be a tough decision. With inside information on over 34 competive Northeastern schools, *New England Colleges* provides the same high-quality information prospective students expect from College Prowler in one all-inclusive, easy-to-use reference.

Schools of the South

Headin' down south? This book will help you find your way to the perfect school!

SCHOOLS OF THE SOUTH
7¼" X 10", 773 Pages Paperback
$29.95 Retail
1-59658-503-X

Southern pride is always strong. Whether it's across town or across state, many Southern students are devoted to their home sweet home. *Schools of the South* offers an honest student perspective on 36 universities available south of the Mason-Dixon.

Untangling
the Ivy League

The ultimate book for everything Ivy!

UNTANGLING THE IVY LEAGUE
7¼" X 10", 567 Pages Paperback
$24.95 Retail
1-59658-500-5

Ivy League students, alumni, admissions officers, and other top insiders get together to tell it like it is. *Untangling the Ivy League* covers every aspect—from admissions and athletics to secret societies and urban legends—of the nation's eight oldest, wealthiest, and most competitive colleges and universities.

Tell Us What Life Is Really Like at Your School!

Have you ever wanted to let people know what your college is really like? Now's your chance to help millions of high school students choose the right college.

Let your voice be heard.

Check out ***www.collegeprowler.com*** for more info!

Need More Help?

Do you have more questions about this school? Can't find a certain statistic? College Prowler is here to help. We are the best source of college information out there. We have a network of thousands of students who can get the latest information on any school to you ASAP. E-mail us at info@collegeprowler.com with your college-related questions.

E-Mail Us Your College-Related Questions!

Check out *www.collegeprowler.com* for more details.
1-800-290-2682

Write For Us!
Get published! Voice your opinion.

Writing a College Prowler guidebook is both fun and rewarding; our open-ended format allows your own creativity free reign. Our writers have been featured in national newspapers and have seen their names in bookstores across the country. Now is your chance to break into the publishing industry with one of the country's fastest-growing publishers!

Apply now at ***www.collegeprowler.com***

Contact editor@collegeprowler.com or
call 1-800-290-2682 for more details.

Pros and Cons

Still can't figure out if this is the right school for you?
You've already read through this in-depth guide; why not
list the pros and cons? It will really help with narrowing down
your decision and determining whether or not
this school is right for you.

Pros	Cons
....	....
....	....
....	....
....	....
....	....
....	....
....	....
....	....
....	....
....	....
....	....
....	....

Pros and Cons

Still can't figure out if this is the right school for you?
You've already read through this in-depth guide; why not
list the pros and cons? It will really help with narrowing down
your decision and determining whether or not
this school is right for you.

Pros	Cons
....	....
....	....
....	....
....	....
....	....
....	....
....	....
....	....
....	....
....	....
....	....
....	....
....	....

Notes

....

....

....

....

....

....

....

....

....

....

....

....

....

Notes

....

....

....

....

....

....

....

....

....

....

....

....

....

Notes

....

....

....

....

....

....

....

....

....

....

....

....

....

Notes

....

....

....

....

....

....

....

....

....

....

....

....

....

Notes

Notes

....

....

....

....

....

....

....

....

....

....

....

....

....

Notes

....

....

....

....

....

....

....

....

....

....

....

....

....

....

Notes

Notes

Notes

....

....

....

....

....

....

....

....

....

....

....

....

....

Notes

....

....

....

....

....

....

....

....

....

....

....

....

....

....

Notes

....

....

....

....

....

....

....

....

....

....

....

....

....

Notes

....

....

....

....

....

....

....

....

....

....

....

....

....

....

Notes

....

....

....

....

....

....

....

....

....

....

....

....

....

Notes

....

....

....

....

....

....

....

....

....

....

....

....

....

Notes

....

....

....

....

....

....

....

....

....

....

....

....

....

Notes

....

....

....

....

....

....

....

....

....

....

....

....

....

Notes

....

....

....

....

....

....

....

....

....

....

....

....

....

Notes

....

....

....

....

....

....

....

....

....

....

....

....

....

Notes

Notes

Notes

Notes

....

....

....

....

....

....

....

....

....

....

....

....

....

Notes

Notes

....

....

....

....

....

....

....

....

....

....

....

....

....

Notes

Notes

···
···
···
···
···
···
···
···
···
···
···
···
···
···